TEACHER'S PET PUBLICATIONS

LITPLAN TEACHER PACK
for
Fever 1793
based on the book by
Laurie Halse Anderson

Written by
Christina Stone

© 2007 Teacher's Pet Publications
All Rights Reserved

Copyright Teacher's Pet Publications 2007

Only the student materials in this unit plan (such as worksheets,
study questions, and tests) may be reproduced multiple times
for use in the purchaser's classroom.

For any additional copyright questions,
contact Teacher's Pet Publications.

www.tpet.com

TABLE OF CONTENTS – *Fever 1793*

Introduction	5
Unit Objectives	7
Reading Assignment Sheet	8
Unit Outline	9
Study Questions (Short Answer)	13
Quiz/Study Questions (Multiple Choice)	27
Pre-reading Vocabulary Worksheets	49
Lesson One (Introductory Lesson)	65
Oral Reading Evaluation Form	77
Writing Assignment 1	79
Writing Evaluation Form	80
Nonfiction Assignment Sheet	83
Writing Assignment 2	90
Writing Assignment 3	99
Extra Writing Assignments/Discussion ?s	102
Vocabulary Review Activities	112
Unit Review Activities	113
Unit Tests	117
Unit Resource Materials	155
Vocabulary Resource Materials	177

A FEW NOTES ABOUT THE AUTHOR

Laurie Halse Anderson was born in upstate New York. Her maiden name, Halse, is often mispronounced; it rhymes with waltz.

Laurie was turned on to writing in the second grade during a haiku lesson. She read all the time, enjoying historical fiction, science fiction, and fantasy more than any other genres. She also had an interest in foreign cultures and languages. In high school, Laurie moved out of her parent's house and lived on a pig farm in Denmark where she was an exchange student.

After her high school graduation, Laurie worked for minimum wage in a clothing store, where she quickly discovered she needed to go college. She attended Onondaga Community College for two years, working on a dairy farm milking cows during that time. She later transferred to Georgetown University and graduated with a degree in Languages and Linguistics. Laurie got married after graduating from college; she and her husband then had two daughters.

Laurie never thought of writing as a career, but later became a freelance reporter. Though she was sent several rejection letters, she eventually published some nonfiction and children's storybooks.

In 1999, Laurie published *Speak*, which won several awards. She then published *Fever 1793*, several books that are part of the *Wild at Heart* series, *Prom, Catalyst*, a companion novel to *Speak*, and *Twisted,* which was published in 2007.

Recently, Laurie and her husband divorced; she is now remarried and part of a great extended family.

INTRODUCTION

This LitPlan has been designed to develop students' reading, writing, thinking, and language skills through exercises and activities related to *Fever 1793*. It includes twenty-two lessons, supported by extra resource materials.

The **introductory lesson** creates a coffeehouse simulation in the classroom, getting students to think about the purposes they serve. This introduces students to a primary setting in the novel. Following the transition, students are given the materials they will be using during the unit. At the end of the lesson, students begin the pre-reading work for the first reading assignment.

The **reading assignments** are approximately 35-40 pages each; some are a little shorter while others are a little longer. Students have approximately 15 minutes of pre-reading work to do prior to each reading assignment. This pre-reading work involves reviewing the study questions for the assignment and doing some vocabulary work for 10 vocabulary words they will encounter in their reading.

The **study guide questions** are fact-based questions; students can find the answers to these questions right in the text. These questions come in two formats: short answer or multiple choice. The best use of these materials is probably to use the short answer version of the questions as study guides for students (since answers will be more complete), and to use the multiple choice version for occasional quizzes.

The **vocabulary work** is intended to enrich students' vocabularies as well as to aid in the students' understanding of the book. Prior to each reading assignment, students will complete a two-part worksheet for approximately 10 vocabulary words in the upcoming reading assignment. Part I focuses on students' use of general knowledge and contextual clues by giving the sentence in which the word appears in the text. Students are then to write down what they think the words mean based on the words' usage. Part II nails down the definitions of the words by giving students dictionary definitions of the words and having students match the words to the correct definitions based on the words' contextual usage. Students should then have an understanding of the words when they meet them in the text.

After each reading assignment, students will go back and formulate answers for the study guide questions. Discussion of these questions serves as a **review** of the most important events and ideas presented in the reading assignments.

After students complete reading the work, there is a **vocabulary review** lesson which pulls together all of the fragmented vocabulary lists for the reading assignments and gives students a review of all of the words they have studied.

Following the vocabulary review, a lesson is devoted to the **extra discussion questions/writing assignments**. These questions focus on interpretation, critical analysis, and personal response, employing a variety of thinking skills and adding to the students' understanding of the novel.

There is a **project** in this unit. This project requires students to keep a journal modeled after the format of the novel.

There are three **writing assignments** in this unit, each with the purpose of informing, persuading, or expressing personal opinions. The first writing assignment asks students to talk about their dreams, like Matilda often does in the novel. The second writing assignment gives students several roles from which to write, all informing someone about the situation in Philadelphia during the outbreak of yellow fever. The third writing assignment asks students to persuade someone to get involved with a humanitarian organization and help others like Matilda does in the novel.

There is a nonfiction **reading assignment**. Students must read nonfiction articles, books, etc. to gather information about their themes in our world today.

The **review lesson** pulls together all of the aspects of the unit. The teacher is given four or five choices of activities or games to use which all serve the same basic function of reviewing all of the information presented in the unit.

The **unit test** comes in two formats: multiple choice or short answer. As a convenience, two different tests for each format have been included. There is also an advanced short answer unit test for advanced students.

There are additional **support materials** included with this unit. The **Unit Resource Materials** section includes suggestions for an in-class library, crossword and word search puzzles related to the novel, and extra worksheets. There is a list of **bulletin board ideas** which gives the teacher suggestions for bulletin boards to go along with this unit. In addition, there is a list of **extra class activities** the teacher could choose from to enhance the unit or as a substitution for an exercise the teacher might feel is inappropriate for his/her class. **Answer keys** are located directly after the **reproducible student materials** throughout the unit. The **Vocabulary Resource Materials** section includes similar worksheets and games to reinforce the vocabulary words.

The **level** of this unit can be varied depending upon the criteria on which the individual assignments are graded, the teacher's expectations of his/her students in class discussions, and the formats chosen for the study guides, quizzes and test. If teachers have other ideas/activities they wish to use, they can usually easily be inserted prior to the review lesson.

The student materials may be reproduced for use in the teacher's classroom without infringement of copyrights. No other portion of this unit may be reproduced without the written consent of Teacher's Pet Publications, Inc.

UNIT OBJECTIVES – *Fever 1793*

1. Through reading Laurie Halse Anderson's novel *Fever 1793*, students will analyze growth in an individual while thinking about principles in both modern and historic societies.

2. Students will demonstrate their understanding of the text on four levels: factual, interpretive, critical, and personal.

3. Students will make connections with the material in the text and apply the lessons learned to their lives.

4. Students will be given the opportunity to practice reading aloud and silently to improve their skills in each area.

5. Students will answer questions to demonstrate their knowledge and understanding of the main events and characters in *Fever 1793* as they relate to the author's theme development.

6. Students will enrich their vocabularies and improve their understanding of the novel through the vocabulary lessons prepared for use in conjunction with the novel.

7. The writing assignments in this unit are geared to several purposes:
    a. To have students demonstrate their abilities to inform, to persuade, or to express their own personal ideas
        Note: Students will demonstrate ability to write effectively to <u>inform</u> by developing and organizing facts to convey information. Students will demonstrate the ability to write effectively to <u>persuade</u> by selecting and organizing relevant information, establishing an argumentative purpose, and by designing an appropriate strategy for an identified audience. Students will demonstrate the ability to write effectively to <u>express personal ideas</u> by selecting a form and its appropriate elements.
    b. To check the students' reading comprehension
    c. To make students think about the ideas presented by the novel
    d. To encourage logical thinking
    e. To provide an opportunity to practice good grammar and improve students' use of the English language.

8. Students will read aloud, report, and participate in large and small group discussions to improve their public speaking and personal interaction skills.

READING ASSIGNMENT SHEET – *Fever 1793*

Date Assigned	Pages Assigned	Completion Date
	Assignment #1 Chapters 1-5	
	Assignment #2 Chapters 6-10	
	Assignment #3 Chapters 11-16	
	Assignment #4 Chapters 17-21	
	Assignment #5 Chapters 22-25	
	Assignment #6 Chapters 26-Epilogue	

UNIT OUTLINE - *Fever 1793*

1 Introduction Activity Project Assignment PVR1	2 Study Quest. 1 Appendix Guided Notes	3 Learning about the time period PVR2	4 Study Quest. 2 Oral Reading Evaluation PVR3	5 Writing Assignment #1
6 Study Quest. 3 Dealing with tough times	7 Nonfiction Assignment PVR4	8 Study Quest. 4 "The Masque of the Red Death"	9 "The Masque of the Red Death" Cont. Venn Diagram PVR5	10 Study Quest. 5 Economic Disparity PVR6
11 Study Quest. 6 Writing Assignment #2	12 Exploring character	13 Time line of Matilda's growth Modern Tragedies	14 Speaker	15 Humanitarian Group Research
16 Writing Assignment #3	17 Group work for humanitarian organization Extra Discussion Questions	18 Extra Discussion Questions Cont. Finish group work for humanitarian organization	19 Letter to the Author Unit Reaction	20 Vocabulary Review
21 Unit Review Project Due	22 Unit Test			

Key: P = Preview Study Questions V = Vocabulary Work R = Read

STUDY GUIDE QUESTIONS

SHORT ANSWER STUDY GUIDE QUESTIONS – *Fever 1793*

Assignment #1
Chapters 1-5
1. Where does Matilda live?
2. What business does Matilda's family own?
3. Who is Silas?
4. What historical event sparked an increase in Matilda's family business?
5. What happened to Matilda's father?
6. Who is King George?
7. Eliza is a black woman living freely. Explain how she is treated in society and how she was able to earn her freedom.
8. What future does Matilda dream of for herself?
9. Why doesn't Polly show up for work?
10. Describe the atmosphere of Matilda's family business in the afternoon.
11. What rumor is circulating through the city?
12. Why is Matilda's mother thinking of sending her to live with a family friend in the country?
13. How does Matilda's mother feel about the boy Matilda has a crush on?
14. Aside from telling the time, why do the church bells ring?
15. How is the community dealing with the many deaths that have been occurring?

Assignment #2
Chapters 6-10
1. Matilda's family earns extra profits from the coffeehouse in August, but no one can agree on how to spend it. Discuss the opinions of all three family members on how the money should be spent.
2. Matilda's grandfather refuses to believe that the deaths are related to yellow fever. Who does he blame for the weird sickness circulating through the city?
3. Matilda's mother and grandfather have different views regarding the spread of a fever. What does Matilda's mother want to do? What does her grandfather want to do?
4. What grand idea does Matilda have to get more business at the coffeehouse?
5. Why is Matilda's mother so eager to have tea with Mrs. Ogilvie?
6. How do the Ogilvie daughters regard Matilda?
7. Describe the differences in lower, middle, and upper-class people in Matilda's city.
8. Matilda starts to think that maybe going to live on a farm in the country wouldn't be that bad after all. What prompts her to change her mind?
9. What do Matilda and her grandfather encounter on their walk home from the printer?
10. What symptoms of illness does Matilda's mother have?
11. Why does Matilda's mother yell at her to leave?
12. Once the doctor diagnosis Matilda's mother with yellow fever, what method of treatment does he try?

Fever 1793 Study Questions page 2

13. Matilda's grandfather has finally decided it is time to flee the city to get away from the spread of yellow fever. Why can't Matilda's mother travel with them?
14. What package does Matilda receive?
15. How is Matilda's grandfather dressed when they leave the city?

Assignment #3
Chapters 11-16
1. As Matilda and her grandfather are traveling to the country with the farmer and his family, they come across four men on horseback. Initially, who do they think these men are?
2. How do Matilda and her grandfather end up stranded?
3. What trick does Matilda use to find water for her and her grandfather?
4. Why does Matilda's grandfather call himself a fool?
5. While stranded on the side of the road Matilda's grandfather says, "We must form our battle plans, both for this skirmish and for the rest of the war." What does he mean by this?
6. What does Matilda use to try to catch fish?
7. After gathering fresh pears, Matilda heads back to feed and care for her grandfather. What happens on the way back?
8. Who is Mrs. Flagg?
9. What is Bush Hill?
10. Why is Matilda terrified to be at Bush Hill?
11. What does Matilda's grandfather do while she is recovering at Bush Hill?
12. The clerk at Bush Hill discharges Matilda since she is once again healthy. Where does he want to send her?
13. What do the workers at Bush Hill want Matilda to do once she is discharged?
14. Describe Philadelphia when Matilda and her grandfather return.
15. Where does Matilda think her mother is?

Assignment #4
Chapters 17-21
1. What do Matilda and her grandfather discover when they enter the coffeehouse for the first time?
2. What is Matilda relieved to find hidden under a stair?
3. How often does Matilda usually bathe?
4. How does Matilda's grandfather feel about leaving the house to find food?
5. What does Matilda plan to do at the end of each day?
6. How does Matilda help her grandfather the night they are being robbed?
7. What are Matilda's grandfather's last words?
8. Why is it fitting that Matilda's grandfather be buried in his nightshirt?
9. What item does Matilda bury with her grandfather?
10. How does Matilda get the men to allow a prayer to be said before burying her grandfather?
11. What does Matilda find when she goes to the market for food?

Fever 1793 Study Questions page 3

12. Why does Matilda go to the newspaper printer?
13. Who is Nell?
14. Why is Matilda searching for Reverend Allen's group?
15. Who does Matilda reunite with?

Assignment #5
Chapters 22-25
1. What was Eliza's first question for Matilda?
2. Who is Joseph?
3. What does Matilda learn about her mother from Eliza?
4. Why does Dr. Rush want the black people to help care for fever victims?
5. Matilda is helping out at Eliza's house, acting more like an adult with each passing day. Give three ways Matilda is acting like a mature adult.
6. Why does Matilda decide to hurry up and take Nell to the orphan house?
7. Describe the orphanage.
8. What does Matilda find out about Colette Ogilvie?
9. What falls from the sky as Eliza and Matilda are walking home?
10. Who is hidden behind the shutters in the house Matilda and Eliza pass on their way home?
11. Why is it difficult for farmers to come to Philadelphia to sell food?
12. What odd ingredient are the people of Philadelphia putting in their bread?
13. Who is making a profit off the yellow fever?
14. Once William, Robert, and Nell come down with yellow fever, Matilda suggests that Eliza take them to Bush Hill. Eliza refuses. Where does Matilda suggest instead?
15. Why is Matilda so against calling a doctor to help William, Robert, and Nell?

Assignment #6
Chapters 26-Epilogue
1. Why do Eliza and Matilda drag all the furniture outside to the garden?
2. What does Joseph bring the boys and Nell when he comes to visit?
3. Why does Matilda go to the market?
4. What are the prices at the market?
5. Nathaniel stayed locked in a house with his employer, Mr. Peale, during the plague. Since they never left or let anyone enter, how did they survive with the food shortage?
6. Why is Matilda annoyed at all the people returning from the country?
7. What does Matilda enjoy at the end of each day?
8. Why hasn't Matilda received a letter from her mother?
9. What chore do Matilda and Eliza give to the children to keep them busy and out of trouble?
10. What does Joseph want Matilda do to with the coffeehouse?
11. Why does Matilda need a lawyer to make Eliza a full partner of the coffeehouse?
12. What does the messenger bring during Thanksgiving dinner?

Fever 1793 Study Questions page 4

13. Describe business at the coffeehouse.
14. People have been returning to Philadelphia and the town is coming alive once again. What event sparks a massive return to the city for all the remaining people in the country?
15. What has happened to Matilda's mother?

ANSWER KEY SHORT ANSWER STUDY GUIDE QUESTIONS – *Fever 1793*

Assignment #1
Chapters 1-5

1. Where does Matilda live?
    Matilda lives in Philadelphia.

2. What business does Matilda's family own?
    Matilda lives with her mother and grandfather. They own Cook's Coffeehouse.

3. Who is Silas?
    Silas is the cat that lives with Matilda.

4. What historical event sparked an increase in Matilda's family business?
    When George Washington built a house only two blocks away, the business at the coffeehouse greatly improved.

5. What happened to Matilda's father?
    He fell off a ladder and died of a broken neck several years ago.

6. Who is King George?
    King George is a parrot that was won on a bet. He hangs in a cage at the coffeehouse and repeats bits of conversation.

7. Eliza is a black woman living freely. Explain how she is treated in society and how she was able to earn her freedom.
    Since she is black, Eliza is treated differently than white people; however, she is still free to do what she wants. Eliza used to be a slave until her husband earned enough money to buy her freedom. She describes that day as the best day of her life.

8. What future does Matilda dream of for herself?
    Matilda dreams of traveling to France to bring back beautiful fabric, combs, and jewelry to sell in her own dry goods store. She also dreams of owning a whole block of other businesses including a restaurant, apothecary, school, and hatter's shop.

9. Why doesn't Polly show up for work?
    When Polly is late to work everyone assumes she is flirting with the boy she likes. The family later finds out that Polly died of a fever in the night.

10. Describe the atmosphere at Matilda's family business in the afternoon.
    The coffeehouse is busy with people from various professions. They gather to discuss news and politics, and they sometimes gamble.

11. What rumor is circulating through the city?
    People in the city are saying that a fever is plaguing people, and it is originating from the area around the docks.

12. Why is Matilda's mother thinking of sending her to live with a family friend in the country?
    Matilda's mother is worried about the rumors of a fever in the city. She feels like Matilda would be safer living in the country away from the possibility of disease.

13. How does Matilda's mother feel about the boy Matilda has a crush on?
    Matilda's mother does not like Nathaniel Benson. She feels like he has no future and is not a suitable match for her daughter. She tells Matilda not to walk by the place where he works, and she always tries to keep Matilda away from him when he comes to the coffeehouse.

14. Aside from telling the time, why do the church bells ring?
    The church bells ring to signify another death in the city. They ring once for each year the person lived.

15. How is the community dealing with the many deaths that have been occurring?
    Many people are worried and talking about fleeing the city to go to the country. Others deny that there is any problem or place the blame on people who are sinners or foreigners.

Assignment #2
Chapters 6-10

1. Matilda's family earns extra profits from the coffeehouse in August, but no one can agree on how to spend it. What are the opinions of all three family members as to how the money should be spent?
   Matilda's grandfather wants to open a store with the extra money, Matilda wants to buy new equipment for the coffeehouse and try to expand their store into a full restaurant, and Matilda's mother wants to save the money because she fears yellow fever will take over the town and hurt business.

2. Matilda's grandfather refuses to believe that the deaths are related to yellow fever. Who does he blame for the weird sickness circulating through the city?
   Matilda's grandfather blames the refugees, or foreigners, for bringing disease.

3. Matilda's mother and grandfather have different views regarding the spread of a fever. What does Matilda's mother want to do? What does her grandfather want to do?
    Matilda's mother wants to flee to the country to avoid getting sick, but Matilda's grandfather doesn't believe the sickness is yellow fever. He wants to keep running the coffeehouse and try to earn a big profit.

4. What grand idea does Matilda have to get more business at the coffeehouse?
    Matilda wants to see if Thomas Jefferson will eat at the coffeehouse and maybe even President George Washington and his wife. She thinks if they eat there business will be booming.

5. Why is Matilda's mother so eager to have tea with Mrs. Ogilvie?
    She is happy to be invited into an upper-class woman's house, and she is hoping that Mrs. Ogilvie's son Edward will be interested in marrying Matilda.

6. How do the Ogilvie daughters regard Matilda?
    They look at her like a lower-class person. They stick their tongues out at her, prevent her from enjoying the snacks, and insult her family's business.

7. Describe the differences in lower, middle, and upper-class people in Matilda's city.
    The lower-class people have nowhere to go to get any type of health care. They are crammed into areas by the wharf and are just waiting to die. Many people blame the illness on them. The middle-class people are stuck in the middle. They can get a doctor, but are still uncertain whether to leave their businesses or stay to try and earn more money. The upper-class people have fled to their country homes to avoid getting sick.

8. Matilda starts to think that maybe going to live on a farm in the country wouldn't be that bad after all. What prompts her to change her mind?
    After Matilda and her grandfather visit the printer's shop, Matilda begins to think that maybe her family should go to the country for a while. The men in the shop are talking about how several hundred have already died and are discussing the new warning from the mayor. This scares Matilda and makes her think her family would be safer elsewhere.

9. What do Matilda and her grandfather encounter on their walk home from the printer?
    On their way home from the printer they see a man pushing a cart with a woman's arm hanging out. It turns out to be Matilda's mother being dumped off at her house. She fell ill while out in the town.

10. What symptoms of illness does Matilda's mother have?
    Her eyes have turned a yellow color, she has a fever, she is tired, she has convulsions, she is vomiting blood, and a foul-smelling black liquid is coming out of her body.

11. Why does Matilda's mother yell at her to leave?
    Matilda's mother is scared her daughter will get sick if she stays with her. She doesn't want her daughter to catch yellow fever from her, so she yells at her to leave instead of taking care of her.

12. Once the doctor diagnoses Matilda's mother with yellow fever, what method of treatment does he try?
    The doctor decides to bleed her mother. He cuts her arm open and wait for her blood to fill up a basin.

13. Matilda's grandfather has finally decided it is time to flee the city to get away from the spread of yellow fever. Why can't Matilda's mother travel with them?
    Other towns turn away all fever victims. There is no town that will allow her mother to enter.

14. What package does Matilda receive?
    Matilda gets a package from Nathaniel. He sends her one of his painting along with a note telling her he is safe at the Peale's house and hopes she stays safe too.

15. How is Matilda's grandfather dressed when they leave the city?
    Matilda's grandfather is dressed in his old military uniform.

Assignment #3
Chapters 11-16
1. As Matilda and her grandfather are traveling to the country with the farmer and his family, they come across four men on horseback. Initially, who do they think these men are?
    Initially, Matilda and the group she is traveling with think the men on horseback are robbers.

2. How do Matilda and her grandfather end up stranded?
    The men on horseback are actually men with a doctor inspecting visitors for signs of yellow fever before they can enter their city. The men see Matilda's grandfather cough violently and assume he is sick. The farmer they are traveling with throws them out of the wagon and leaves with all of their belongings.

3. What trick does Matilda use to find water for herself and her grandfather?
    Matilda stands on a hill and searches for a willow tree, knowing there will be water nearby.

4. Why does Matilda's grandfather call himself a fool?
    Her grandfather feels his stubborn nature prevented the family from fleeing the city before anyone got sick. He acknowledges that Matilda's mother was right and that they should have left the city long ago.

5. While stranded on the side of the road Matilda's grandfather says, "We must form our battle plans, both for this skirmish and for the rest of the war." What does he mean by this?
    Matilda's grandfather is saying they need a plan for how they will get out of their current situation, being stranded in the country with no food or supplies, and a plan for how they will deal with the threat of yellow fever after they are able to return home.

6. What does Matilda use to try to catch fish?
    Matilda uses her skirt to try and catch fish in the river.

7. After gathering fresh pears, Matilda heads back to feed and care for her grandfather. What happens on the way back?
    Matilda feels cold all over and then passes out.

8. Who is Mrs. Flagg?
    Mrs. Flagg is a nurse at Bush Hill. She is caring for Matilda while she is sick with yellow fever. It seems Matilda's grandfather has a crush on Mrs. Flagg.

9. What is Bush Hill?
    Bush Hill is a mansion that has been converted in a hospital to care for fever victims.

10. Why is Matilda terrified to be at Bush Hill?
    Matilda has heard that Bush Hill is a dangerous place. She heard that it is not respectable and that dead bodies were piled everywhere while thieves preyed on the weak.

11. What does Matilda's grandfather do while she is recovering at Bush Hill?
    Matilda's grandfather keeps busy by organizing the delivery of food to people at Bush Hill, burning filthy mattresses, and helping to create ways to raise money to care for the sick.

12. The clerk at Bush Hill discharges Matilda once she is healthy again. Where does he want to send her?
    The clerk knows that Matilda's father is dead and her mother is unable to be reached. He wants to send Matilda to the orphanage.

13. What do the workers at Bush Hill want Matilda to do once she is discharged?
    They want her to "give back" by working at the orphanage. They want her to care for children who lost their parents to yellow fever and to help out with the cleaning.

14. Describe Philadelphia when Matilda and her grandfather return.
    Instead of returning to the thriving city of Philadelphia, Matilda returns to a place that looks dead. There are dead bodies and trenches of graves everywhere, little food to go around, and the city is no longer safe because of thieves who prey on the weak and dead.

15. Where does Matilda think her mother is?
    Matilda and her grandfather assume that her mother got better and headed out to the country to be with the rest of her family. They assume she is at the Ludington family's farm.

Assignment #4
Chapters 17-21
1. What do Matilda and her grandfather discover when they enter the coffeehouse for the first time?
    Matilda and her grandfather discover the coffeehouse has been robbed.

2. What is Matilda relieved to find hidden under a stair?
    Matilda is happy to find that the thieves did not find the strongbox where her family hid their money.

3. How often does Matilda usually bathe?
    Matilda bathes once a month or for special occasions.

4. How does Matilda's grandfather feel about leaving the house to find food?
    He feels like the city is unsafe and wants to stay at home to rummage for food in the garden until it is absolutely necessary that they leave the house.

5. What does Matilda plan to do at the end of each day?
    Matilda wants to read at the end of each day, specifically from the Bible.

6. How does Matilda help her grandfather the night they are being robbed?
    Matilda's grandfather is being attacked by one of the burglars. Matilda sees her grandfather is losing, so she picks up his sword and stabs the thief in his shoulder.

7. What are Matilda's grandfather's last words?
    His last words are, "Love you."

8. Why is it fitting that Matilda's grandfather is buried in his nightshirt?
    Matilda's grandfather described death as an eternal sleep, so Matilda thinks it is only fitting that he is dressed for sleep.

9. What item does Matilda bury with her grandfather?
    Matilda buries her grandfather with a portrait of her grandmother.

10. How does Matilda get the men to allow a prayer to be said before burying her grandfather?
    Matilda pushes one of the men so hard he almost falls in the grave. She then grabs him by the collar of his shirt and threatens him until he allows her to say a prayer.

11. What does Matilda find when she goes to the market for food?
    Matilda discovers that the market is no longer open. There is no food, and rats are picking at the scraps.

12. Why does Matilda go to the newspaper printer?
    Matilda wants to put an ad in the newspaper to try and find her mother.

13. Who is Nell?
    Nell is a young girl Matilda finds while wandering the city trying to figure out what to do. Nell is in a home crying next to her dead mother who is obviously a fever victim.

14. Why is Matilda searching for Reverend Allen's group?
    When looking for help and someone to care for Nell, a neighbor tells Matilda that women from this group carry a basket of food and can probably find someone to take care of the girl and the remains of her mother.

15. With whom does Matilda reunite?
    Matilda reunites with Eliza.

Assignment #5
Chapters 22-25

1. What was Eliza's first question for Matilda?
   Eliza immediately asks why Matilda is not at the Ludington's farm with her mother.

2. Who is Joseph?
   Joseph is Eliza's brother. He has been sick with the fever. Robert and William are his two sons.

3. What does Matilda learn about her mother from Eliza?
   Matilda learns that her mother recovered from the fever and was headed to the Ludington's farm.

4. Why does Dr. Rush want the black people to help care for fever victims?
   He believes that black people cannot catch yellow fever.

5. Matilda is helping out at Eliza's house, acting more like an adult with each passing day. Give three ways Matilda is acting like a mature adult.
   Matilda is giving up her portion of the food so that the younger children can eat, she is doing chores around the house and taking very little time to rest, she travels with Eliza to help sick people until she is weak from exhaustion, and she tries to do the right thing when it comes to taking care of Nell.

6. Why does Matilda decide to hurry up and take Nell to the orphan house?
    Mother Smith tells Matilda she is being selfish if she keeps loving and caring for Nell. She explains that it will only make it harder for the young child when she has to go to the orphanage. Matilda realizes this is true and decides to take Nell to the orphanage the next day.

7. Describe the orphanage.
    The woman who answers the doors is surrounded by crying children. She explains that with the lack of mail, there is no way to contact any other family members. There is little money, the place is overcrowded, and the children are hungry. She says the orphan house should be a last resort.

8. What does Matilda find out about Colette Ogilvie?
    She hears that while Colette was ill she kept screaming for Louis. It turns out that instead of marrying the man she was already engaged to, she eloped with her French tutor.

9. What falls from the sky as Eliza and Matilda are walking home?
    Daisies fall from the sky as the two walk home. They are actually being thrown down from a window above the street.

10. Who is hidden behind the shutters in the house Matilda and Eliza pass on their way home?
    Nathaniel Benson is in the house, staying hidden behind the shutters.

11. Why is it difficult for farmers to come to Philadelphia to sell food?
    Farmers have trouble getting into the city since more and more places restrict people from traveling into the city.

12. What odd ingredient are the people of Philadelphia putting in their bread?
    The people are putting sawdust in their bread. They mix it with the flour to make it go farther, giving them horrible tasting bread, but something to keep them from hunger.

13. Who is making a profit off the yellow fever?
    The pharmacists are making a huge profit by charging more for medicine needed to treat yellow fever.

14. Once William, Robert, and Nell come down with yellow fever, Matilda suggests that Eliza take them to Bush Hill. Eliza refuses. Where does Matilda suggest instead?
    Matilda suggests they take the sick children to the coffeehouse instead of Bush Hill.

15. Why is Matilda so against calling a doctor to help William, Robert, and Nell?
    Matilda knows the doctor will bleed the children. She feels that the French doctors at Bush Hill are more successful in curing yellow fever, and they do not bleed patients. She suspects bleeding patients makes the sickness worse.

Assignment #6
<u>Chapters 26-Epilogue</u>
1. Why do Eliza and Matilda drag all the furniture outside to the garden?
    There has been a frost overnight and Eliza wants the furniture outside so when another frost comes, the germs on all of the household items will be killed, allowing the house to be rid of yellow fever.

2. What does Joseph bring the boys and Nell when he comes to visit?
    Joseph brings the boys tops to play with and Nell a doll.

3. Why does Matilda go to the market?
    Matilda goes to the market because it has finally reopened and it a great place for gossip. She hopes to hear about her mother from all the returning citizens.

4. What are the prices at the market?
    The prices are very low and there is an abundance of food.

5. Nathaniel stayed locked in a house with his employer, Mr. Peale, during the plague. Since they never left or let anyone enter, how did they survive with the food shortage?
    Mr. Peale collects exotic animals and stuffs them. He kept the meat from all the animals he stuffed, leaving the family meat from possums and other odd animals.

6. Why is Matilda annoyed at all the people returning from the country?
    Matilda feels like they are full of happiness with no thought to the suffering they escaped when they fled.

7. What does Matilda enjoy at the end of each day?
    She enjoys a leisurely walk with Nathaniel every evening.

8. Why hasn't Matilda received a letter from her mother?
    The post office shut down during the outbreak of yellow fever and even though the threat is over and people are returning, the post office is still closed.

9. What chore do Matilda and Eliza give to the children to keep them busy and out of trouble?
    The children are given the butter churn and have to turn milk into butter.

10. What does Joseph want Matilda do to with the coffeehouse?
    Joseph says she needs to sell it so that she has a nice dowry.

11. Why does Matilda need a lawyer to make Eliza a full partner of the coffeehouse?
    Many people in society will think that Eliza, being black, took advantage of the young white girl. Too many people don't like to see black people move up in society, so to be safe they will use a lawyer to make it is official.

12. What does the messenger bring during Thanksgiving dinner?
    A messenger stops by to bring a free sample of coffee beans. He is hoping to gain the business of the coffeehouse by being their supplier.

13. Describe business at the coffeehouse.
    Every chair in the coffeehouse is full. They have expanded their menu and hope to soon expand the business. Matilda has proved to be a very successful businesswoman.

14. People have been returning to Philadelphia and the town is coming alive once again. What event sparks a massive return to the city for all the remaining people in the country?
    When President George Washington returns to the city all the remaining people in the country know it must be safe to come back too.

15. What happened to Matilda's mother?
    She went to the Ludington's farm a few days after Matilda and her grandfather headed there, even thought she was still ill. When she didn't find her daughter there she became frantic and attempted to search for her. She was found on the side of the road near death and now she has become very fragile.

STUDY GUIDE/QUIZ QUESTIONS – *Fever 1793*
Multiple Choice Format

Assignment #1
Chapters 1-5
1. Where does Matilda live?
   A. Philadelphia
   B. Boston
   C. New York
   D. Pittsburgh

2. What business does Matilda's family own?
   A. A small printing shop
   B. A restaurant
   C. A coffeehouse
   D. A dry goods store

3. Who is Silas?
   A. A businessman friend of Matilda's grandfather
   B. A cat that lives with Matilda
   C. A free black man who helps with running the family business
   D. A character in Matilda's favorite book

4. What historical event sparked an increase in Matilda's family business?
   A. A huge battle took place during the War of Independence right outside the business, making it a historical landmark.
   B. George Washington built his home a few blocks away.
   C. Someone was murdered just outside the front door, bringing lots of press, gossip, and business.
   D. All the businesses near the water had to close due to the fever, making people come further into the city.

5. What happened to Matilda's father?
   A. He was killed by the fever.
   B. He moved to another city to try and open his business in another location.
   C. He fell off a ladder and broke his neck, causing him to die.
   D. He went bankrupt and was put in a prison for people who owed debt.

Fever 1793 Multiple Choice Questions for Assignment 1 page 2

6. Who is King George?
    A. A parrot won in a card game
    B. The new king of Great Britain who wants to regain control in America
    C. An old friend of Matilda's grandfather
    D. A horse that Matilda's grandfather loses while gambling

7. What is Eliza's living situation like?
    A. Her husband was able to buy her out of slavery, making her a free black. She is still treated differently than white people, but is free.
    B. She is a slave owned by Matilda's family. She is trying to buy her way out of slavery.
    C. Her husband was able to buy her out of slavery, making her a free black. She is treated with the same respect as white people.
    D. She is a slave owned by Matilda's family and is happy with her life since they treat her with respect and kindness.

8. What future does Matilda dream of for herself?
    A. She wants to be married to a rich and noble gentleman.
    B. She wants to travel to France and one day own several businesses of her own.
    C. She wants to move to the country where she can enjoy the scenery and fresh air.
    D. She wants to take over the family business and eventually pass it on to her children.

9. Why doesn't Polly show up for work?
    A. She hears rumor about the fever and is too scared to leave the house.
    B. Her parents decided she is to marry an wealthy man who can support her.
    C. She was too busy flirting with Matthew, the blacksmith's son.
    D. She died overnight due to a fever.

10. Describe the atmosphere at Matilda's family business in the afternoon.
    A. The business has slowed down since most people are at work.
    B. The business is closed to clean up from the lunch crowd and prepare for the upcoming dinner crowd.
    C. The business is packed with people talking about politics and news.
    D. The business is full of children wanting after school snacks.

11. What rumor is circulating through the city?
    A. Matilda will soon be married to Nathaniel Benson.
    B. The British people are planning another attack.
    C. A fever is plaguing people, and it is originating from the area around the docks.
    D. The market is suffering because the weather has been so dry.

Fever 1793 Multiple Choice Questions for Assignment 1 page 3

12. Why is Matilda's mother thinking of sending her to live with a family friend in the country?
    A. Her mother is afraid that Matilda will catch the fever and die if she stays in the city.
    B. Her mother is worried Matilda will try to run off with Nathaniel Benson.
    C. Her mother is tired of Matilda's attitude and laziness and wants to punish her.
    D. Her mother cannot support her any longer due to the rising cost of owning a business.

13. How does Matilda's mother feel about the boy Matilda has a crush on?
    A. She likes him and thinks it is a good match.
    B. She thinks he is going nowhere in life and is therefore not a suitable match.
    C. She fears he is too old for her daughter and will die much sooner than Matilda.
    D. She thinks he is too easily angered and may end up hurting her daughter.

14. Aside from telling the time, why do the church bells ring?
    A. To signify the start of another church service
    B. To signify someone has just given birth
    C. To signify someone has just been married
    D. To signify another person has died

15. How is the community dealing with the many deaths that have been occurring?
    A. People are very sad and upset, wearing all black to show they are in mourning.
    B. Many people don't believe a fever is spreading. They say those who are dying are sinners or the deaths are just a coincidence.
    C. They are all fleeing to the country to avoid the possibility of death and the city is becoming abandoned.
    D. They are trying to find doctors from other cities to help treat people and figure out a cure for the fever.

Fever 1793 Multiple Choice Questions for Assignment 2

Assignment #2
Chapters 6-10

1. Matilda's family earns extra profits from the coffeehouse in August, but no one can agree on how to spend it. Which of the following correctly expressing the wishes of ALL THREE family members?
    A. Matilda wants to use it to expand the coffeehouse into a restaurant, her grandfather wants to save the money, and her mother wants to use it to go to the country.
    B. Matilda wants to use it to open a store, her grandfather wants to use it to travel to the country and her mom wants to save it.
    C. Matilda wants save it for a trip to France, her grandfather wants to save it, and her mother wants to expand the coffeehouse into a restaurant.
    D. Matilda wants to expand the coffeehouse into a restaurant, her grandfather wants to open a store, and her mother wants to save it.

2. Matilda's grandfather refuses to believe that the deaths are related to yellow fever. Who does he blame for the weird sickness circulating through the city?
    A. The refugees and foreigners
    B. The sailors who just came back from Europe
    C. The lower class women
    D. The British government

3. Which of the following correctly expresses how BOTH Matilda's mother and grandfather feel about the spread of disease?
    A. Matilda's mother and grandfather both feel safe in the city as long as they stay away from the wharves.
    B. Matilda's mother wants to go to the country and her grandfather wants to stay in the city.
    C. Matilda's mother wants to stay in the city and her grandfather wants to go to the country.
    D. Matilda's mother and grandfather both want to go to the country for safety.

4. What grand idea does Matilda have to get more business at the coffeehouse?
    A. Have doctors eat at the coffeehouse to help give customers advice on how to stay safe from the spreading disease.
    B. Have Thomas Jefferson and President George Washington eat at the coffeehouse to attract customers.
    C. Have a huge party with all the upper-class people of society to attract customers who will spend more money.
    D. Convince the wagon driver who takes people out to the country to pick up at their coffeehouse so people will stop there and spend money before leaving.

Fever 1793 Multiple Choice Questions for Assignment 2 page 2

5. Why is Matilda's mother so eager to have tea with Mrs. Ogilvie?
    A. She hasn't been invited to a party since the death of her husband.
    B. She wants Matilda to be friends with Mrs. Ogilvie's daughters.
    C. She is excited to eat the delicious food that will be served.
    D. She wants Matilda to become engaged to Mrs. Ogilvie's son.

6. How do the Ogilvie daughters regard Matilda?
    A. They stick their tongues out at her, prevent her from eating, and insult her.
    B. They insult her at first but then invite her to come back again after they got to know her.
    C. They compliment her at first but then stick their tongue out at her after they hear Matilda's mother talk.
    D. They compliment her hair, give her a small gift, and invite her to come back.

7. Which of the following correctly describes the differences between the lower, middle, and upper-class people in Matilda's city?
    A. The lower-class have no where to get health care, the middle-class can't decide whether to leave their businesses or stay to make money, and the upper-class flee to the country for safety.
    B. The lower-class are all dying quickly, the middle-class are able to get health care and survive without any problems, and the upper-class are fleeing to the country.
    C. The lower-class are fleeing to the country, the middle-class can't decide whether to leave their businesses or stay to make money, and the upper-class can afford good health care while remaining in the city.
    D. The lower-class are all dying quickly, the middle-class are fleeing to the country, and the upper-class can afford good heath care while remaining in the city.

8. Matilda starts to think that maybe going to live on a farm in the country wouldn't be that bad after all. What prompts her to change her mind?
    A. After hearing Eliza tell her about the news she got from the Free African Society meeting, she wants to leave.
    B. After seeing Colette Ogilvie collapse from fever, she wants to leave.
    C. After seeing her mother suffer from yellow fever, she wants to leave.
    D. After hearing at the printers that several hundred people in her city have already died, she wants to leave.

9. What do Matilda and her grandfather encounter on their walk home from the printer?
    A. Several dead bodies of fever victims piled in the street
    B. Matilda's mother being dumped out of a cart, apparently sick with the fever
    C. A group people with the fever begging for money, food, and help
    D. Eliza lying on the side of the road trying to get home, apparently sick with the fever

Fever 1793 Multiple Choice Questions for Assignment 2 page 3

10. What symptoms of illness does Matilda's mother have?
    A. Yellow eyes, more energy than ever, loss of memory, and a fever
    B. Yellow eyes, blood in her vomit, convulsions, and a fever
    C. Yellow eyes, sores on her body, a bad taste in her mouth, and a fever
    D. Yellow eyes, difficulty breathing, loss of hearing, and a fever

11. Why does Matilda's mother yell at her to leave?
    A. She is embarrassed for Matilda to see her this sick.
    B. She is angry at Matilda for not taking good enough care of her.
    C. She is worried Matilda might catch the fever from her.
    D. She is nervous the family will lose money if Matilda doesn't run the coffeehouse.

12. Once the doctor diagnoses Matilda's mother with yellow fever, what method of treatment does he try?
    A. Giving her plenty of fluids and requiring she take a bath every four hours
    B. Cutting open her arm and bleeding her to get the sickness out
    C. Pouring ice on her body to bring down the fever
    D. Giving her antibiotics to fight the disease

13. Matilda's grandfather has finally decided it is time to flee the city to get away from the spread of yellow fever. Why can't Matilda's mother travel with them?
    A. She is too confused to understand and refuses to go.
    B. Travel is expensive, and there isn't enough money for all three people to go.
    C. Other towns won't allow people with yellow fever to enter.
    D. She is too sick to travel; it would surely kill her.

14. What package does Matilda receive?
    A. A painting and a note from Nathaniel
    B. A package of small treats and a note from Mrs. Ogilvie to come visit again
    C. A new smock from Eliza to wear while she is in the country
    D. A knife from her grandfather to protect herself on the journey to the country

15. How is Matilda's grandfather dressed when they leave the city?
    A. With a yellow bandana to symbolize someone in the family has yellow fever
    B. In all black to mourn the sickness of Matilda's mother
    C. In his old military uniform, sword and all
    D. In very old clothes, making him look poor

Fever 1793 Multiple Choice Questions for Assignment 3

Assignment #3
Chapters 11-16
1. As Matilda and her grandfather are traveling to the country with the farmer and his family, they come across four men on horseback. Initially, who do they think these men are?
    A. Robbers
    B. Doctors
    C. Fever victims
    D. Soldiers

2. How do Matilda and her grandfather end up stranded?
    A. The wagon they are traveling in has a broken axle, and no one has the money to make the repair.
    B. The roads are all closed to reduce the spread of fever. The family they are traveling with decides to head back while Matilda and her grandfather decide to find another way.
    C. The men on horseback think Matilda's grandfather has yellow fever, so they refuse to let him in the town. The family dumps them on the road and goes on without them.
    D. Two people in the family they are traveling with get yellow fever. Matilda and her grandfather fear for their lives and decide to wait on the road for another wagon.

3. What trick does Matilda use to find water for her and her grandfather?
    A. She uses her skirt and canteen to collect the rain water.
    B. She looks at the bottom of a hill, knowing that is where water collects.
    C. She follows the birds and squirrels, knowing they are heading to water.
    D. She looks for a willow tree, knowing water will be nearby.

4. Why does Matilda's grandfather call himself a fool?
    A. He knows his old army tricks won't help them survive in this situation.
    B. He knows he should have listened to Matilda's mother and left Philadelphia a lot sooner than they did.
    C. He left the city knowing he had yellow fever and is afraid he will give it to Matilda.
    D. He didn't bring enough food to last them the whole trip, and now they are in danger of starving.

Fever 1793 Multiple Choice Questions for Assignment 3 page 2

5. While stranded on the side of the road Matilda's grandfather says, "We must form our battle plans, both for this skirmish and for the rest of the war." What does he mean by this?
    A. That he and Matilda not only need to figure out how to get off the roadside, but also what they will do to survive and get their lives back together.
    B. That he and Matilda not only need to figure out how to get back to her mother, but also how to find a cure for yellow fever.
    C. That he and Matilda not only need to figure out how to get the clothing back, but also how to increase business at the coffeehouse.
    D. That he and Matilda not only need to find a way home, but also how to get Matilda a good husband.

6. What does Matilda use to try to catch fish?
    A. A fishing pole she finds by a tree
    B. A basket she makes from branches
    C. Her grandfather's sword
    D. Her skirt

7. After gathering fresh pears, Matilda heads back to feed and care for her grandfather. What happens on the way back?
    A. Matilda kills a rabbit with her grandfather's sword.
    B. Matilda sees a victim of yellow fever and tries to help him.
    C. Matilda comes across two men who try to rob her of her food.
    D. Matilda feels cold all over and passes out.

8. Who is Mrs. Flagg?
    A. The wife of a farmer who takes in Matilda and her grandfather
    B. A nurse who is helping Matilda recover from yellow fever
    C. A woman Matilda meets who is dying from yellow fever
    D. The wife of a farmer who gives Matilda food and clothing

9. What is Bush Hill?
    A. The hill where Matilda and her grandfather are stranded
    B. A cemetery where Matilda suspects her mother was buried
    C. A mansion converted into a hospital to care for yellow fever victims
    D. The dry goods store where Matilda and her grandfather are able to get food

Fever 1793 Multiple Choice Questions for Assignment 3 page 3

10. Why is Matilda terrified to be at Bush Hill?
    A. She has heard it is a dangerous place full of thieves.
    B. She is terrified by how dirty the area is and thinks she might get sick.
    C. She knows if she is there she will probably die.
    D. She sees a man get murdered and fears for her own life.

11. What does Matilda's grandfather do while she is recovering at Bush Hill?
    A. Delivers food, burns dirty mattresses, and helps figure out how to raise more money
    B. Carries dead bodies to the fire where they are cremated
    C. Helps children who lost their parents to yellow fever find a new home
    D. Hangs out in the barn trying to recover from his own illness

12. The clerk discharges Matilda since she is once again healthy. Where does he want to send her?
    A. Back to Philadelphia
    B. To an orphanage
    C. To the Ludington's farm
    D. To train to become a nurse

13. What do the workers at the hospital want Matilda to do once she is discharged?
    A. Take care of her grandfather, making sure he takes his medicine three times a day
    B. Help transport dead bodies for burial
    C. Give back to the community by getting a job helping in the orphanage
    D. Help her grandfather get the coffeehouse up and running again

14. Describe Philadelphia when Matilda and her grandfather return.
    A. There is little food, and the city is no longer safe.
    B. Most people have returned from the country, and businesses are open once again.
    C. The city has fire damage since people burned houses of the dead to end the fever.
    D. Almost everyone is homeless since most businesses are now hospitals.

15. Where does Matilda think her mother is?
    A. At the Ludington's farm
    B. Dead
    C. Staying with Eliza
    D. Working at a hospital to help fever victims

Fever 1793 Multiple Choice Questions for Assignment 4

Assignment #4
Chapters 17-21
1. What do Matilda and her grandfather discover when they enter the coffeehouse for the first time upon their return?
    A. The coffeehouse is a mess from a recent robbery.
    B. They find a note Eliza left informing them Matilda's mother had passed away.
    C. The coffeehouse is thriving with doctors and nurses on break from treating victims.
    D. They find a note from Matilda's mother telling them she went to the Ludington's farm.

2. What is Matilda relieved to find hidden under a stair?
    A. Her cat, Silas
    B. The painting Nathaniel sent to her before she left
    C. A strongbox where money was hidden
    D. Extra preserves that Eliza had stored for an emergency

3. How often does Matilda usually bathe?
    A. Once a day
    B. Once a week
    C. Once a month
    D. Once a year

4. How does Matilda's grandfather feel about leaving the house to find food after they return?
    A. He feels like the city is safe enough for Matilda to take a quick trip to the market.
    B. He feels like the city is only safe for a man, and he won't let Matilda go.
    C. He feels like the city is only safe for a healthy person like Matilda.
    D. He feels like the city is unsafe for them both and wants to rummage for food in the garden first.

5. What does Matilda plan to do at the end of each day?
    A. Read the Bible
    B. Take a bath
    C. Make sure the house is clean
    D. Think of her mother

6. How does Matilda help her grandfather the night they are being robbed?
    A. She takes her grandfather's rifle and shoots the robber.
    B. She tells the robber where the money is hidden, and he stops hurting her grandfather.
    C. She takes her grandfather's sword and stabs the robber.
    D. She causes a commotion to distract the robber so her grandfather can get away.

Fever 1793 Multiple Choice Questions for Assignment 4 page 2

7. What are Matilda's grandfather's last words?
    A. Keep fighting
    B. Take care
    C. Love you
    D. Good work soldier

8. Why is it fitting that Matilda's grandfather would be buried in his nightshirt?
    A. He always said death was the eternal sleep, so he should be buried in his nightshirt.
    B. He was most comfortable in his nightshirt, so he should be buried in it to really rest in peace.
    C. He would have wanted her to sell his clothing for extra money, so he should be buried in his nightshirt since it wouldn't sell for as much as his other clothes.
    D. He died in the middle of the night, so it seemed right to let him be buried in what he was wearing.

9. What item does Matilda bury with her grandfather?
    A. A Bible
    B. His chess set
    C. The sword he used while in the army
    D. A portrait of her grandmother

10. How does Matilda get the men to allow a prayer to be said before burying her grandfather?
    A. She offers them a few potatoes from the garden so they will have something to eat.
    B. She begins to sob, and the men feel bad since she is a young girl.
    C. She begs and pleads and reminds them that they would have prayed if it were their family.
    D. She pushes one of the men and grabs him by his shirt to threaten him.

11. What does Matilda find when she goes to the market for food?
    A. Some of the farmers have ventured back, but the prices are too much for her to afford.
    B. The market has been turned into a hospital, and fever victims are everywhere.
    C. There is no food anywhere, only rats picking at scraps.
    D. Life is getting back to normal, and the regular sellers are finally back.

12. Why does Matilda go to the newspaper printer?
    A. To place an obituary in for her grandfather
    B. To look in the classifieds to try and find work
    C. To place an ad to try and find her mother
    D. To see if she can work there

Fever 1793 Multiple Choice Questions for Assignment 4 page 3

13. Who is Nell?
    A. A poor woman who has just lost three of her children to the fever
    B. A little girl Matilda finds crying next to her dead mother
    C. A woman sick with the fever who reminds Matilda of her mother
    D. A small dog that seems to have a broken leg

14. Why is Matilda searching for Reverend Allen's group?
    A. She is told they can help her find someone to care for Nell.
    B. She thinks they will take her in and care for her now that she is alone.
    C. She is told they have information about people who died from the fever, and she hopes they can tell her whether or not her mother is still alive.
    D. She thinks that maybe they can officially bless her grandfather's grave.

15. With whom does Matilda reunite?
    A. Her mother
    B. Nathaniel
    C. Eliza
    D. King George

Fever 1793 Multiple Choice Questions for Assignment 5

Assignment #5
Chapters 22-25

1. What was Eliza's first question for Matilda?
    A. How her grandfather's health is
    B. Why she isn't with her mother at the Ludington's farm
    C. If she had heard her mother passed away
    D. If she has seen what happened to the coffeehouse

2. Who is Joseph?
    A. Eliza's husband
    B. A leader in Reverend Allen's group
    C. Eliza's brother
    D. The boy Matilda was supposed to marry

3. What does Matilda learn about her mother from Eliza?
    A. Her mother recovered from the fever and headed to the farm.
    B. Her mother recovered from the fever and is helping care for fever victims.
    C. Her mother had trouble recovering and was sent to Bush Hill.
    D. Her mother did not recover and passed away.

4. Why does Dr. Rush want the black people to help care for fever victims?
    A. He thinks it is a way to repay the white people for allowing them their freedom.
    B. He knows the black people have to do everything the white people say so they cannot argue or refuse.
    C. He hates black people and hopes they will catch the fever too.
    D. He thinks black people are immune to yellow fever.

5. Matilda is helping out at Eliza's house, acting more like an adult with each passing day. In what three ways is Matilda acting like a mature adult?
    A. She legally adopted Nell, is working to restore the coffeehouse, and is considering getting married.
    B. She gives up her portion of food to feed the children, asks for extra chores, and is helping care for fever victims.
    C. She is cooking all the meals, caring for all three children by herself, and working to restore the coffeehouse.
    D. She is learning to sew and mend clothing, considering marriage, and taking a leadership role in Reverend Allen's organization.

Fever 1793 Multiple Choice Questions for Assignment 5 page 2

6. Why does Matilda decide to hurry up and take Nell to the orphan house?
    A. She feels overworked caring for a child that is not hers. She knows it is not her responsibility to watch over Nell.
    B. She feels angered by the way Nell has been acting. She is causing trouble in Eliza's house and becoming a burden for everyone.
    C. She hears a rumor that Nell may have family in a neighboring city. She knows the orphan house will help her reunite with her distant relatives.
    D. She feels like she is being selfish. The longer she takes care of Nell, the harder it will be for the young child to be separated from Matilda.

7. What is the situation at the orphan house?
    A. It is overcrowded and running low on money. There are not enough people to care for all the children and food is running low.
    B. Yellow fever is starting to plague the small children. A sick child was brought in by mistake and passed the disease on to most of the other children.
    C. The workers are finding homes for the children with relatives elsewhere. Hardly any children are labeled as orphans since the workers can quickly contact other relatives.
    D. It has closed down. There is a sign on the door directing people to orphanages in safer cities.

8. What does Matilda find out about Colette Ogilvie?
    A. She created a family scandal by eloping with her French tutor.
    B. She told her brother about Matilda's visit, and now he is no longer interested in marrying her.
    C. She lost all of her family and is now living in the mansion alone.
    D. She passed away from yellow fever after fainting the day Matilda visited.

9. What falls from the sky as Eliza and Matilda are walking home?
    A. Feathers
    B. Daisies
    C. Rain
    D. Snow

10. Who is hidden behind the shutters in the house Matilda and Eliza pass on their way home?
    A. Nathaniel Benson
    B. Colette Ogilvie
    C. Mrs. Flagg
    D. Dr. Rush

Fever 1793 Multiple Choice Questions for Assignment 5 page 3

11. Why is it difficult for farmers to come to Philadelphia to sell food?
    A. Farmers have caught the fever too and several are dying, leaving few left to help harvest the food to sell in the city.
    B. Animals are now getting sick with the fever, leaving almost no meat for anyone.
    C. Farmers do not have enough help to take care of their crops, and the drought is killing almost everything, leaving no leftover food to take to the city.
    D. Farmers are not allowed to travel in and out of the city due to restrictions placed by the government to help avoid spreading the fever.

12. What odd ingredient are the people of Philadelphia putting in their bread?
    A. Potatoes
    B. Ashes from coals after a fire
    C. Sawdust
    D. Insect repellent

13. Who is making a profit off the yellow fever?
    A. The black people
    B. Hospitals
    C. Pharmacists and apothecaries
    D. Owners of large wagons

14. Once William, Robert, and Nell come down with yellow fever, Matilda suggests that Eliza take them to Bush Hill. Eliza refuses. Where does Matilda suggest instead?
    A. The coffeehouse
    B. The Ludington's farm
    C. A hospital like Bush Hill, but much closer
    D. The Ogilvie mansion

15. Why is Matilda so against calling a doctor to help William, Robert, and Nell?
    A. She knows that Eliza and her family will not have the money to pay. She doesn't want them to sacrifice their home in order to get help.
    B. She knows he will bleed the children. After seeing how the French doctors at Bush Hill treated patients, she realizes that bleeding only makes the fever worse.
    C. She knows that several doctors are really uneducated. Several are drunks who can do nothing to help.
    D. She knows that the doctors will try to take advantage of a young girl and a black woman, so she fears they may regret the decision later.

Fever 1793 Multiple Choice Questions for Assignment 6

Assignment #6
Chapters 26-Epilogue
1. Why do Eliza and Matilda drag all the furniture outside to the garden?
    A. They are forced to stay out the garden since the house is too hot.
    B. They want the coffeehouse to look empty from the street so no one else will rob it.
    C. They want to kill all the yellow fever germs by placing it outside for the next frost.
    D. They need to wash it all off, and that will be easier to do in the garden next to the well.

2. What does Joseph bring the boys and Nell when he comes to visit?
    A. Food
    B. Toys
    C. Medicine
    D. Clean clothes

3. Why does Matilda go to the market?
    A. To get food before Eliza and the children die of starvation
    B. To try and hear if there is any news about her mother
    C. To look for Nathaniel
    D. To get out of the house and away from the sick children

4. What are the prices at the market?
    A. Very high since the market has just reopened and people are desperate for food
    B. Moderate since farmers know the people of Philadelphia have suffered so much
    C. Very low since there is plenty of food
    D. Variable since some farmers are desperate for money while others are more charitable

5. Nathaniel stayed locked in a house with his employer, Mr. Peale, during the plague. Since they never left or let anyone enter, how did they survive with the food shortage?
    A. Mr. Peale had such a thriving garden, the family could eat the vegetables for several months.
    B. Mr. Peale had live chickens and horses in his parlor room. He killed them when the family needed more meat.
    C. Mr. Peale collected and stuffed exotic animals. He saved the meat from the animals before he stuffed them so the family ate odd animals like possums.
    D. Mr. Peale dug an underground tunnel. He hired farmers to smuggle food to him through the tunnel.

Fever 1793 Multiple Choice Questions for Assignment 6 page 2

6. Why is Matilda annoyed at all the people returning from the country?
    A. She feels like they are happy, well-fed, and giving no thought to the suffering anyone else endured.
    B. She feels like they are bragging about how rich they are and how much fun it was to take a vacation from the city; she is a little jealous.
    C. She hears them saying bad things about black people and gets defensive since she has been living in the black community for the last couple of months.
    D. She liked the city when it wasn't so crowded and noisy.

7. What does Matilda enjoy at the end of each day?
    A. A hot cup of fresh coffee
    B. A piece of whatever dessert Eliza has made
    C. Taking a walk with Nathaniel
    D. Reading Nell a bedtime story

8. Why hasn't Matilda received a letter from her mother?
    A. Her mother is dead.
    B. Her mother cannot write and therefore cannot send a letter.
    C. The post office is closed.
    D. Eliza is secretly stealing her mail.

9. What chore do Matilda and Eliza give to the children to keep them busy and out of trouble?
    A. Picking flowers to set on the table for Thanksgiving dinner
    B. Rolling up a big ball of string
    C. Getting water from the well to take care of the garden
    D. Using the butter churn to turn milk into butter

10. What does Joseph want Matilda do to with the coffeehouse?
    A. Sell it so she can use the money to follow her dreams and go to Paris
    B. Sell it so she will have money for a dowry to get married
    C. Keep it and try to restore it to the successful business it once was
    D. Give it to him so that he can restore it to the successful business it once was

Fever 1793 Multiple Choice Questions for Assignment 6 page 3

11. Why does Matilda need a lawyer to make Eliza a full partner of the coffeehouse?
    A. Matilda is drawing up a complicated plan that will make Eliza a partner. However, the first several years of her profits will go straight to Matilda until she has paid for her half of the coffeehouse. Since this may be confusing, a lawyer is needed to keep it straight.
    B. There is worry about what will happen if Matilda's mother comes back or Matilda changes her mind. In order to make sure Eliza gets what she deserves, a lawyer is needed to make permanent changes.
    C. With the establishment of the new American government, there is now a law requiring all business owners to register and pay taxes. A lawyer is needed to make sure the proper paperwork is filled out.
    D. Too many people will think that Eliza, being black, took advantage of the young, white girl. White people don't usually like to see black people move up in society and to avoid any trouble, a lawyer is needed to make it official.

12. What does the messenger bring during Thanksgiving dinner?
    A. A letter from Matilda's mother
    B. Flowers from Nathaniel
    C. A free sample of coffee beans
    D. News that Matilda's mother is dead

13. Describe business at the coffeehouse.
    A. Every chair in the coffeehouse is full. They have expanded the menu, and Matilda has proven to be a very successful businesswoman.
    B. Business is starting to pick up. The coffeehouse is not full, but Eliza and Matilda are able to support themselves.
    C. Business is slow since many people have not yet returned from the country.
    D. The business has gone bankrupt, and Matilda will have to marry in order to survive.

14. People have been returning to Philadelphia, and the town is coming alive once again. What event sparks a massive return to the city for all the remaining people in the country?
    A. When the market reopens, that is a sign that the fever is over and people are safe to return to the city.
    B. When President George Washington returns to the city, all the remaining people in the country know it must be safe to return, too.
    C. When there is a town meeting called, everyone knows it is safe to return form the country.
    D. When the first heavy snowfall comes at Christmas, people know the fever is gone.

Fever 1793 Multiple Choice Questions for Assignment 6 page 4

15. What has happened to Matilda's mother?
    A. She went to the Ludington's farm a few days after Matilda and her grandfather headed there, even thought she was still ill. When she didn't find her daughter, she became frantic and attempted to search for her. She was found on the side of the road near death and now she has become very fragile.
    B. She tried to make it to the Ludington's farm but was not allowed into the city since she still had traces of yellow fever. Friends eventually went looking for her and found her half dead on the side of the road. She now has serious health problems with her heart.
    C. She was able to make it to the Ludington's farm, but when the rest of the household caught yellow fever she was not able to fight off the disease and passed away.
    D. She passed away before she ever left Philadelphia.

ANSWER KEY - MULTIPLE CHOICE STUDY/QUIZ QUESTIONS
Fever 1793

	1-5	6-10	11-16	17-21	22-25	26-Epilogue
1	A	D	A	A	B	C
2	C	A	C	C	C	B
3	B	B	D	C	A	B
4	B	B	B	D	D	C
5	C	D	A	A	B	C
6	A	A	D	C	D	A
7	A	A	D	C	A	C
8	B	D	B	A	A	C
9	D	B	C	D	B	D
10	C	B	A	D	A	B
11	C	C	A	C	D	D
12	A	B	B	C	C	C
13	B	C	C	B	C	A
14	D	A	A	A	A	B
15	B	C	A	C	B	A

PREREADING VOCABULARY WORKSHEETS

VOCABULARY Chapters 1-5 *Fever 1793*

Part I: Using Prior Knowledge and Contextual Clues

Below are the sentences in which the vocabulary words appear in the text. Read the sentence. Use any clues you can find in the sentence combined with your prior knowledge, and write what you think the underlined words mean on the lines provided.

1. Instead he jumped on Mother's quilt and prepared to pick apart his breakfast. Mother's best quilt. Mother <u>abhorred</u> mice.
   _____

2. I could see the masts of the ships tied up at the <u>wharves</u> on the Delaware River.
   _____

3. If not for Eliza's fine <u>victuals</u>, and the hungry customers who paid to eat them, we'd have been in the streets long ago.
   _____

4. "I bet she's dawdling by the <u>forge</u>," I said, "watching Matthew work with his shirt collar open."
   _____

5. He tried to <u>instill</u> some military training in me.
   _____

6. It's the source of a deadly <u>miasma</u>, a foul stench, indeed.
   _____

7. Mary Shewall died soon after of a <u>bilious</u> fever, and one could hardly fault her character.
   _____

8. And do not let me hear of you <u>loitering</u> shamelessly in front of the Peale house.
   _____

9. He snatched an apple from my basket and took a bite. The <u>impudence</u>.
   _____

10. I would fish like a lady, with good posture and a <u>demure</u> manner.
    _____

Fever 1793 Vocabulary Worksheet Chapters 1-5 Continued

Part II: Determining the Meaning
   Match the vocabulary words to their dictionary definitions.

___ 1. abhorred   A. the workshop of a blacksmith
___ 2. wharves   B. extremely unpleasant or distasteful in regards to sickness
___ 3. victuals   C. landing places where ships may tie up and load or unload
___ 4. forge   D. poisonous fumes or germs polluting the atmosphere
___ 5. instill   E. lingering aimlessly; hanging about with no purpose
___ 6. miasma   F. shy, modest, coy, or reserved
___ 7. bilious   G. detested utterly; loathed; hated
___ 8. loitering   H. the quality of being offensively bold; nerve; rudeness
___ 9. impudence   I. to gradually put something into someone's mind or feelings
___ 10. demure   J. food fit for humans to eat

VOCABULARY Chapters 6-10 *Fever 1793*

Part I: Using Prior Knowledge and Contextual Clues

Below are the sentences in which the vocabulary words appear in the text. Read the sentence. Use any clues you can find in the sentence combined with your prior knowledge, and write what you think the underlined words mean on the lines provided.

1. Silas yowled. Eliza and Grandfather burst into laughter. "Very droll," I said.

2. "I'll tend to this matter, Ladies…Don't bestir yourselves."

3. As soon as I conceded defeat, Mother turned her attention to the most important issue.

4. He prohibits French, no matter how much I implore him.

5. Eliza harrumphed and set the pudding over the fire.

6. Grandfather says this trouble will soon be over. He says people don't have gumption anymore.

7. Men who stood unafraid before British cannon run in fear from this foul pestilence.

8. Sir, I protest most vehemently!

9. Her face was pulled taut in pain, and she jerked in her sleep.

10. No amount of cajoling would change her mind.

Fever 1793 Vocabulary Worksheet Chapters 6-10 Continued

Part II: Determining the Meaning
   Match the vocabulary words to their dictionary definitions.

___ 1. droll   A. offered brief, critical comments
___ 2. bestir   B. yielded, admitted, relinquished, or acknowledged reluctantly
___ 3. conceded   C. tightly drawn or tense
___ 4. implore   D. a deadly disease
___ 5. harrumphed   E. amusing or funny in an odd way
___ 6. gumption   F. with great passion or energy
___ 7. pestilence   G. persuading by using flattery or promises
___ 8. vehemently   H. to beg urgently
___ 9. taut   I. aggressiveness; boldness
___ 10. cajoling   J. to stir up, rouse, or bring to action

VOCABULARY Chapters 11-16 *Fever 1793*

Part I: Using Prior Knowledge and Contextual Clues

Below are the sentences in which the vocabulary words appear in the text. Read the sentence. Use any clues you can find in the sentence combined with your prior knowledge, and write what you think the underlined words mean on the lines provided.

1. Grandfather stopped coughing and leaned back wearily.
   _____

2. "Go ahead," the man said. "Make haste."
   _____

3. I could never abide rotted fruit. It drew flies.
   _____

4. A melodious name for a beautiful lady.
   _____

5. They told of good people who refused to take any money for helping strangers, even though they were poor and near destitute.
   _____

6. "You have hunger?" he asked me. "Yes," I answered. "I'm famished."
   _____

7. My voice as too weak to carry far, and the doctor was already concentrating on the next jaundiced face.
   _____

8. I think he secretly enjoyed the commotion.
   _____

9. I cannot care for this little snippet of a girl.
   _____

10. "It is good that you have each other," said Mrs. Bowles in the same placid voice.
    _____

Fever 1793 Vocabulary Worksheet Chapters 11-16 Continued

Part II: Determining the Meaning
    Match the vocabulary words to their dictionary definitions.

___ 1. wearily   A. sweet sounding
___ 2. haste   B. having a yellow discoloration of the skin due to disease
___ 3. abide   C. swiftness of motion; hurry; rush
___ 4. melodious   D. extremely hungry; starved
___ 5. destitute   E. a small or insignificant person
___ 6. famished   F. acting fatigued, tired, worn out
___ 7. jaundiced   G. quiet; calm; peaceful
___ 8. commotion   H. disturbance; constant activity; chaotic movement
___ 9. snippet   I. to accept or to put up with; to tolerate
___ 10. placid   J. lacking the necessities of life

VOCABULARY Chapters 17-21 *Fever 1793*

Part I: Using Prior Knowledge and Contextual Clues

Below are the sentences in which the vocabulary words appear in the text. Read the sentence. Use any clues you can find in the sentence combined with your prior knowledge, and write what you think the underlined words mean on the lines provided.

1. Grandfather was picking through the broken chairs in the front room, trying to salvage something to sit on.

2. Maybe they saw the fever rag and thought there was still an invalid in the house.

3. I don't want to hear any more talk of venturing outside, unless it's to the garden.

4. Would anyone bother with a trifling robbery when there was death at every door?

5. & 6. The tall one would not relent. He pressed ahead, continuing to brandish the sword back and forth wildly.

7. They wrapped the cloth around him and quickly sewed the shroud shut.

8. A horse was tethered by the door.

9. They charge exorbitant prices for their wares, and get whatever they ask.

10. I hoisted her high in my arms and started south.

Fever 1793 Vocabulary Worksheet Chapters 17-21 Continued

Part II: Determining the Meaning
   Match the vocabulary words to their dictionary definitions.

___ 1. salvage   A. to shake or wave a weapon
___ 2. invalid   B. excessive; extreme; unreasonable
___ 3. venturing   C. small; insignificant; of little importance
___ 4. trifling   D. held by a rope or restraint in a short radius
___ 5. relent   E. raised up; to lifted
___ 6. brandish   F. someone who is too weak to care for himself
___ 7. shroud   G. slack; abandon; withdraw; become more mild
___ 8. tethered   H. taking a risk or braving dangers
___ 9. exorbitant   I. a cloth or sheet in which a corpse is wrapped for burial
___ 10. hoisted   J. saving or rescuing the good of what is left

VOCABULARY Chapters 22-25 *Fever 1793*

Part I: Using Prior Knowledge and Contextual Clues

Below are the sentences in which the vocabulary words appear in the text. Read the sentence. Use any clues you can find in the sentence combined with your prior knowledge, and write what you think the underlined words mean on the lines provided.

1. She led me up the stairs to a small set of rooms, <u>dimly</u> lit, but clean-smelling and orderly.

2. She hugged them tightly before <u>disentangling</u> herself from four arms.

3. Robert, William, and Nell sat on a log and watched me, <u>solemn</u> as three old preachers.

4. She <u>cackled</u> out loud when I tried to comb the knots out of Nell's hair.

5. When the story was over, the boys <u>trundled</u> off to bed without protest.

6. He's a <u>scurrilous</u> dog, that man.

7. Joseph, what <u>ails</u> you? Are you feverish again? Are you chilled?

8. "He'll be fine, and those babies will be fine," said Mother Smith <u>resolutely</u>.

9. & 10. She dosed the boys regularly and gently to <u>purge</u> the <u>putrid</u> bile from their bodies, but it seemed to have little effect.

Fever 1793 Vocabulary Worksheet Chapters 22-25 Continued

Part II: Determining the Meaning
   Match the vocabulary words to their dictionary definitions.

___ 1. dim   A. serious; not to be taken lightly
___ 2. disentangling   B. not bright; dull
___ 3. solemn   C. in the state of foul decay; rotten
___ 4. cackled   D. moved along
___ 5. trundled   E. causes physical or emotional pain
___ 6. scurrilous   F. unraveling; becoming free
___ 7. ails   G. obscene, abusive, vulgar
___ 8. resolutely   H. cleanse; purify
___ 9. purge   I. voiced a shrill, broken laugh
___ 10. putrid   J. with firm resolve or determination

VOCABULARY Chapters 26-Epilogue *Fever 1793*

Part I: Using Prior Knowledge and Contextual Clues
    Below are the sentences in which the vocabulary words appear in the text. Read the sentence. Use any clues you can find in the sentence combined with your prior knowledge, and write what you think the underlined words mean on the lines provided.

1. The fetid stench that had hung over the city for weeks was gone, replaced with brittle, pure air.
   _____

2. The bone-grinding fatigue and numbing hunger of the past weeks evaporated.
   _____

3. Yellow fever had certainly done away with vanity.
   _____

4. Those of us who had remained behind were gaunt and pale.
   _____

5. I'm to ask for the proprietor of Cook's.
   _____

6. "The doctors say it's a miracle she survived at all." "Bunkum," Mother said.
   _____

7. She didn't think they were old enough to do anything besides raise a ruckus in the garden.
   _____

8. A lamplighter some blocks down reached up with his long pole to extinguish the street lamp.
   _____

9. She didn't begrudge me a few minutes of quiet, but the table-setting came first.
   _____

10. These solitary minutes each morning were fast becoming a habit.
    _____

Fever 1793 Vocabulary Worksheet Chapters 26-Epilogue Continued

Part II: Determining the Meaning
   Match the vocabulary words to their dictionary definitions.

___ 1. fetid   A. insincere or ridiculous talk
___ 2. fatigue   B. owner of a business establishment
___ 3. vanity   C. alone or unattended
___ 4. gaunt   D. weariness from bodily or mental exhaustion
___ 5. proprietor   E. to envy or resent the good fortune of someone else
___ 6. bunkum   F. extremely thin and bony
___ 7. ruckus   G. excessive pride in one's appearance
___ 8. extinguish   H. to put out or bring to an end
___ 9. begrudge   I. having an offensive odor
___ 10. solitary   J. a noisy commotion or disturbance

VOCABULARY ANSWER KEY *Fever 1793*

	1-5	6–10	11-16	17-21	22-25	26-Epilogue
1	G	E	F	J	B	I
2	C	J	C	F	F	D
3	J	B	I	H	A	G
4	A	H	A	C	I	F
5	I	A	J	G	D	B
6	D	I	D	A	G	A
7	B	D	B	I	E	J
8	E	F	H	D	J	H
9	H	C	E	B	H	E
10	F	G	G	E	C	C

DAILY LESSONS

LESSON ONE

Objectives
1. To introduce the *Fever 1793* unit
2. To distribute books, study questions, and other related materials
3. To preview the vocabulary and study questions for Assignment #1
4. To begin Assignment #1

Activity #1
Have a few tables in the front of the room with small snacks and coffee. Allow students to get a cup of coffee and a snack as they enter the room. Once everyone has a cup of coffee and something to snack on, begin asking students what the purpose of coffee shops are. Push them to think about what activities take place at coffee shops like Starbucks, Barnie's Coffee, Seattle's Best, or other coffee shops in your community (internet usage, community/group meetings, friends gathering to catch up, music/entertainment, etc). Talk about how those places are regular meeting spots or hangouts for a lot of people at various times in the morning, day, and night.

Transition: Once you have discussed the purposes and functions of coffee shops, tell students they are about to begin reading *Fever 1793*. Tell students that the novel takes place in Philadelphia when that was the capitol of America. Talk about how the main character, Matilda, works at the coffeehouse her family owns. Discuss the importance of coffeehouses during that time, pointing out that they were a place of great popularity. Inform students that coffeehouses were a place where prestigious people gathered to discuss politics and news. Show students the front of the novel, pointing out that there is a girl with yellow eyes. Explain to them that the yellow eyes are a symptom of yellow fever, a deadly disease that plagued Philadelphia. You may also want to explain that the novel is classified as historical fiction, meaning that the names and story are made up, but based on facts and real events in that time.

Activity #2
Show students how each chapter in the novel begins with a quote from someone famous in that time. Talk about how the quote is a lead-in to the material discussed in that chapter. Next, distribute the Words of Wisdom project. Tell students they will be keeping a journal like Matilda does, and starting it off with a quote as well. Discuss the directions in detail.

Activity #3
Distribute the materials students will use in this unit. Explain in detail how students are to use these materials.

Study Guides Students should read the study guide questions for each reading assignment prior to beginning the reading assignment to get a feeling for what events and ideas are important in the section they are about to read. After reading the section, students will (as a class or individually) answer the questions to review the important events and ideas from that section of the book. Students should keep the study guides as study materials for the unit test. **Preview the study questions for chapters 1-5 while students have their guides out.**

Vocabulary Prior to reading a reading assignment, students will do vocabulary work related to the section of the book they are about to read. Following the completion of the reading of the book, there will be a vocabulary review of all the words used in the vocabulary assignments. Students should keep their vocabulary work as study materials for the unit test. **Do the vocabulary worksheet for chapters 1-5 orally to show students how the worksheets are to be done.**

Reading Assignment Sheet You need to fill in the Reading Assignment Sheet to let students know by when their reading has to be completed. You can either write the assignment sheet up on a side blackboard or bulletin board and leave it there for students to see each day, or you can "ditto" copies for each student to have. In either case, you should advise students to become very familiar with the reading assignments so they know what is expected of them.

Extra Activities Center The Unit Resource Materials portion of this LitPlan contains suggestions for an extra library of related books and articles in your classroom as well as crossword and word search puzzles. Make an extra activities center in your room where you will keep these materials for students to use. (Bring the books and articles in from the library and keep several copies of the puzzles on hand.) Explain to students that these materials are available for students to use when they finish reading assignments or other class work early.

Nonfiction Assignment Sheet Explain to students that they each are to read at least one non-fiction piece from the in-class library at some time during the unit. Students will fill out a Nonfiction Assignment Sheet after completing the reading to help you (the teacher) evaluate their reading experiences and to help the students think about and evaluate their own reading experiences.

Books Each school has its own rules and regulations regarding student use of school books. Advise students of the procedures that are normal for your school. Preview the book. Look at the covers, frontmatter, and index.

Activity #5
Tell students that they should read Assignment #1 prior to the next class period. Give them the remainder of this class (if time remains) to complete this assignment.

Words of Wisdom Project

Each chapter in *Fever 1793* begins with a quote from a prominent historical figure of the time. The quote serves as a description for what is taking place in the society as a whole and as a description for what Matilda will talk about in the upcoming chapter in relation to her own life.

You will be keeping a journal recording the events of your daily life just as Matilda does in the novel. Each entry should begin with a quote from a prominent person in today's society, followed by a narrative of your day.

Project Requirements:
- Cover: Take a sheet of construction paper to use as your cover. Write your name in the center of the paper. Next, cut words, phrases, and pictures out of magazines and newspapers that represent you and your personality. Arrange these cutouts in a collage fashion around your name. The cover should be a creative expression of your personality.
- Quotes: Each entry will begin with a quote from a prominent person in today's society. You will have a total of 20 journal entries, so you will need a total of 20 quotes. When selecting your quote each day, try to find one that relates to what you will be talking about in your journal entry. The quote does not need to refer to exactly what you are writing about, but another reader should be able to see the correlation between the quote you select and the journal entry about your day. It may be easier to write the journal entry first, then search for a quote you feel relates to your day. The quote should always be at the start of your journal entry, standing out like it does in the novel. Be sure to copy the quote exactly as it was originally said, citing the person who said it at the end. At least three of your quotes should come from lyrics of music you listen to, three from books or poems from this time period, and three from people currently involved in politics. The remainder of your quotes can be from these categories or any others that you choose, but remember they should be from people of this time period.
- Entries: You will have a total of 20 journal entries. Each journal entry should be at least one full page. You may type the journal entries or write them by hand. Remember to not only recount the events of your day, but also how you felt about what happened. Analyze how the events of the day impacted your life. Talk about your feelings and thoughts as well as the events that took place during the day. Your journal entries should include content that is appropriate for school.
- Organization: Once you have finished all 20 of your journal entries, place them in chronological order. Be sure your writing is neat and readable. Staple the cover you created to the front of your journal entries.

LESSON TWO

Objectives
1. To review main ideas, events, and vocabulary of reading Assignment #1
2. To help students understand the time period the novel in which the novel takes place

Activity #1

Give students a few minutes to formulate answers for the study questions for Assignment #1 and then discuss the answers to the questions in detail. Write the answers on the board or overhead transparency so students can have the correct answers for study purposes.

NOTE: It is a good practice in public speaking and leadership skills for individual students to take charge of leading the discussions of the study questions. Perhaps a different student could go to the front of the class and lead the discussion each day that the study questions are discussed in this unit. Of course, you should guide the discussion when appropriate and try to fill in any gaps students may leave. The study questions could really be handled in a number of different ways, including in small groups with group reports following. Occasionally you may want to use the multiple choice questions as quizzes to check students' reading comprehension. As a short review now and then, students could pair up for the first (or last, if you have time left at the end of a class period) few minutes of class to quiz each other from the study questions. Mix up methods of reviewing the materials and checking comprehension throughout the unit so students don't get bored just answering the questions the same way each day. Variety in methods will also help address the different learning styles of your students. From now on in this unit, the directions will simply say, "Discuss the answers to the study questions in detail as previously directed." You will choose the method of preparation and discussion each day based on what best suits you and your class.

Activity #2

Have students turn to the appendix in the back on the book. These pages will provide students with the necessary background knowledge need to understand Philadelphia in the time period the book takes place.

Place students into small groups of two or three. Hand out the guided reading notes. Assign each group 2-4 sections, depending on the number of students in your class. Instruct each group to read the sections they are assigned and fill in the information needed on their guided reading sheet. Once all the groups have finished their portion of the reading and guided notes, allow groups to go to the front of the class to present their information. Each group should give a short summary of what they read and then guide the class in filling in their guided notes for that portion.

Background Notes for *Fever 1793*

Did the epidemic really happen?
- The epidemic of yellow fever started in _____.
- In _____ months, yellow fever killed _____ percent of Philadelphia's population.
- Thousands of people _____ the city to escape the disease.

Battle of the Doctors
- Both the _____ and the _____ had not been invented for doctors to use at this time.
- At the start of the yellow fever epidemic about _____ doctors were practicing medicine in Philadelphia. Not all of them were properly trained.
- Some people followed Dr. _____. He gave people mercury, calomel, and jalap to make people throw up, hoping to rid their body of disease. He also drained _____ from people's bodies to rid them of the disease. Many people think that his methods actually _____ many of his patients.
- Other people believed the _____ doctors knew how to treat yellow fever. They prescribed rest, fresh air, and lots of fluids. That was and still is the _____ way to treat yellow fever.

Take Two Sponges and Call Me in the Morning
- In a desperate move to cure a disease they knew little about, people would soak sponges in _____ and stick them up their noses. They also used _____ to wash their hair and clothes in. Several even drank it. People hoped this strong liquid would kill all the germs from yellow fever.
- _____ and _____ were shot in the streets in hopes of clearing the air of disease.
- Beds were _____ and then dug up in an effort to kill the disease.
- None of these methods worked. People kept getting sick until the _____ killed off the _____ that spread yellow fever.

Where are they buried?
- Some people are buried in churchyards and cemeteries, but most lie buried _____ in Washington's Square.

The Balloon
- The first hot air balloon was launched in _____ in the city of Philadelphia.
- Everyone in the city stopped what they were doing to watch. The wind blew the balloon _____ miles, making this a very successful scientific experiment. The launch of another flight in the hot air balloon was ruined because of the _____ epidemic.

The Amazing Peale Family
- The Peale family was a real family, although Nathaniel Benson is a fictional character. The family was known as "_____."
- Peale not only had an interest in art; he opened the first _____ museum in his home in the 1780s.
- The two famous explorers, _____ and _____ donated many items from their journey to Mr. Peale.

Free African Society
- The Free African Society was founded in _____ by _____ and _____, who were both born as slaves.
- The Free African Society was a mutual aid organization devoted to helping _____, _____, or _____ African Americans.
- It was also dedicated to abolishing _____.
- During the yellow fever, members of the Free African Society worked to care for all fever victims. After all the charitable work the Free African Society did during the epidemic, they were attacked in a _____ written by _____. He accused them of overcharging for burials and stealing from the sick.
- All the accusations were _____. In response to the attack, the Free African Society published their own pamphlet called _____, which described what the African Americans had done to help their fellow citizens during the epidemic.

Coffeehouses
- Coffeehouses were very popular in this time period. People gathered in them to _____, _____, and _____.
- Owning and running a coffeehouse was a _____ business for a widow.
- The most famous coffeehouse in Philadelphia was called the _____. Several important figures of the time met here frequently.

The French Influence
- The French sent money and aid to help the Americans in the _____.
- By 1793 the French had several problems of their own. America remained _____, but many Americans supported the French.
- Many refuges from France came to America, making French _____ and _____ very popular.
- During the epidemic the _____ doctors had the most effective treatments.

Famous People Touched by the Fever (list each name and give a few details of each)
- _____ :
- _____ :
- _____ :
- _____ :

To Market, To Market
- There were no _____ or _____ to keep food cool during this time, so most people bought their food at the _____.
- _____ would pack their wagons with food and drive into Philadelphia.
- During the yellow fever epidemic, farmers were afraid to come into the city, so getting enough _____ during the epidemic was a problem.
- Most people in the city were without food during the epidemic. Some neighboring towns would _____ food, firewood, and cash to help out.

The Miraculous Moving Capital
- _____ was not the first capital of the country. The capital moved several times before settling there.
- The Continental Congress met for the first time in _____. It was the largest city and centrally located.
- After the government signed a Peace Treaty with the British, the capital was in _____.
- There was much debate about moving the capital, and finally the government decided to settled on the _____ River, which was accessible to many people.
- The government carved out pieces of _____ and _____ so that the capital would not be in just one state, making it unfair.
- _____ was the temporary home for the capital until the capital moved to what is currently Washington DC in 1800.

Fear and Panic
- There had been fevers in Philadelphia before, so most people were _____ when the fevers first began. As the death toll rose, people began to _____.
- The fever closed business and government. Men in handcarts heading to the burial ground yelled out "_____."
- Although it is hard to imagine, many sick people were _____ by their families and thrown into the _____. Kindness seemed to _____.
- The brave people who stayed to help were from the _____, those who worked at _____, and members of the _____. They are the real heroes of this time.

Yellow Fever Today
- Yellow fever still exists, but not in the _____.
- Dr. Walter Reed discovered that _____ spread the disease.
- In the 1930s a vaccine was developed, but yellow fever still kills thousands a year in _____ and parts of _____.

Background Notes Answer Key for *Fever 1793*

Did the epidemic really happen?
- The epidemic of yellow fever started in <u>1793</u>.
- In <u>three</u> months, yellow fever killed <u>10</u> percent of Philadelphia's population.
- Thousands of people <u>fled</u> the city to escape the disease.

Battle of the Doctors
- Both the <u>stethoscope</u> and the <u>thermometer</u> had not been invented for doctors to use at this time.
- At the start of the yellow fever epidemic about <u>80</u> doctors were practicing medicine in Philadelphia. Not all of them were properly trained.
- Some people followed Dr. <u>Rush</u>. He gave people mercury, calomel, and jalap to make people throw up, hoping to rid their body of disease. He also drained <u>blood</u> from people's bodies to rid them of the disease. Many people think that his methods actually <u>killed</u> many of his patients.
- Other people believed the <u>French</u> doctors knew how to treat yellow fever. They prescribed rest, fresh air, and lots of fluids. That was and still is the <u>best</u> way to treat yellow fever.

Take Two Sponges and Call Me in the Morning
- In a desperate move to cure a disease they knew little about, people would soak sponges in <u>vinegar</u> and stick them up their noses. They also used <u>vinegar</u> to wash their hair and clothes in. Several even drank it. People hoped this strong liquid would kill all the germs from yellow fever.
- <u>Guns</u> and <u>cannons</u> were shot in the streets in hopes of clearing the air of disease.
- Beds were <u>buried underground</u> and then dug up in an effort to kill the disease.
- None of these methods worked. People kept getting sick until the <u>frost</u> killed off the <u>mosquitos</u> that spread yellow fever.

Where are they buried?
- Some people are buried in churchyards and cemeteries, but most lie buried <u>anonymously</u> in Washington's Square.

The Balloon
- The first hot air balloon was launched in <u>1793</u> in the city of Philadelphia.
- Everyone in the city stopped what they were doing to watch. The wind blew the balloon <u>15</u> miles, making this a very successful scientific experiment. The launch of another flight in the hot air balloon was ruined because of the <u>yellow fever</u> epidemic.

The Amazing Peale Family
- The Peale family was a real family, although Nathaniel Benson is a fictional character. The family was known as "The First Family of American Art."
- Peale not only had an interest in art; he opened the first natural history museum in his home in the 1780s.
- The two famous explorers, Meriwether Lewis and William Clark, donated many items from their journey to Mr. Peale.

Free African Society
- The Free African Society was founded in 1787 by Richard Allen and Absalom Jones, who were both born as slaves.
- The Free African Society was a mutual aid organization devoted to helping widowed, ill, or out-of-work African-Americans.
- It was also dedicated to abolishing slavery.
- During the yellow fever, members of the Free African Society worked to care for all fever victims. After all the charitable work the Free African Society did during the epidemic, they were attacked in a pamphlet written by Matthew Clarkson. He accused them of overcharging for burials and stealing from the sick.
- All the accusations were lies. In response to the attack, the Free African Society published their own pamphlet called A Narrative of the Proceedings of Black People During the Late Awful Calamity in Philadelphia in 1793, which described what the African Americans had done to help their fellow citizens during the epidemic.

Coffeehouses
- Coffeehouses were very popular in this time period. People gathered in them to conduct business, talk politics, and catch up on the news.
- Owning and running a coffeehouse was a respectable business for a widow.
- The most famous coffeehouse in Philadelphia was called the London Coffee House. Several important figures of the time met here frequently.

The French Influence
- The French sent money and aid to help the Americans in the American Revolution.
- By 1793 the French had several problems of their own. America remained neutral, but many Americans supported the French.
- Many refuges from France came to America, making French fashion and language very popular.
- During the epidemic the French doctors had the most effective treatments.

Famous People Touched by the Fever (list each name and give a few details of each)
- Dolley Payne Todd Madison: first lady of the fourth president; first husband died of yellow fever
- George Washington: his wife, Martha, had a friend who died of yellow fever
- Dr. Benjamin Rush: famous doctor who contracted the disease and survived
- Stephen Girard: transformed Bush Hill into a safe hospital; survived yellow fever

To Market, To Market
- There were no refrigerators or freezers to keep food cool during this time, so most people bought their food at the marketplace.
- Farmers would pack their wagons with food and drive into Philadelphia.
- During the yellow fever epidemic, farmers were afraid to come into the city, so getting enough food during the epidemic was a problem.
- Most people in the city were without food during the epidemic. Some neighboring towns would donate food, firewood, and cash to help out.

The Miraculous Moving Capital
- Washington DC was not the first capital of the country. The capital moved several times before settling there.
- The Continental Congress met for the first time in Philadelphia. It was the largest city and centrally located.
- After the government signed a Peace Treaty with the British, the capital was in New York.
- There was much debate about moving the capital, and finally the government decided to settled on the Potomac River, which was accessible to many people.
- The government carved out pieces of Maryland and Virginia so that the capital would not be in just one state, making it unfair.
- Philadelphia was the temporary home for the capital until the capital moved to what is currently Washington DC in 1800.

Fear and Panic
- There had been fevers in Philadelphia before, so most people were calm when the fevers first began. As the death toll rose, people began to panic.
- The fever closed business and government. Men in handcarts heading to the burial ground yelled out "Bring out your dead."
- Although it is hard to imagine, many sick people were abandoned by their families and thrown into the street. Kindness seemed to evaporate.
- The brave people who stayed to help were from the Free African Society, those who worked at Bush Hill, and members of the Mayors Committee. They are the real heroes of this time.

Yellow Fever Today
- Yellow fever still exists, but not in the United States.
- Dr. Walter Reed discovered that mosquitos spread the disease.
- In the 1930s a vaccine was developed, but yellow fever still kills thousands a year in Africa and parts of South America.

LESSON THREE

Objectives
1. To teach students about the life of people living in the time period in which the novel is set
2. To give students the necessary framework for understanding terminology used in the novel
3. To preview the vocabulary and study questions for Assignment #2
4. To begin Assignment #2

Activity #1

Throughout the novel Matilda mentions several items of clothing. She distinguishes between the clothing she wears as a middle class citizen, the clothing the Ogilvie's wear as upper class citizens, and the clothing Eliza wears as a free black. Matilda also mentions several popular trades of the time. To help students understand the clothing, trades, and lifestyle of the time period, you will need to check out a projector and laptop with internet capabilities from your school library or resource center. (Note: You may want to take your students to a computer lab if that is available within your school. Students could then follow along as you guide them through the activities you want them to do.)

The Colonial Williamsburg web page has great interactive programs available online for you to use in your classroom. Under the clothing tab, there is information about clothing of the time based on class level in society. There is an interactive dress up feature that would be fun for students as well. Under the multimedia tab, there are short videos and slide shows that tell about popular trades during that time. These two areas are most essential for students to understand the clothing and trades Matilda mentions throughout her story. Depending on the resources available at your school and the amount of time you have in a class period, select a few of these activities and videos to show to your class. If you have more time to devote to this activity, there are several wonderful articles, videos, and activities within this page for you and your students to explore. The web page is available at http://www.history.org/history/

Activity #2

Students should complete the vocabulary worksheet and preview the study questions for Assignment #2.

Activity #3

Students should read Assignment #2 prior to the next class period. Give them the remainder of this class (if time remains) to complete this assignment.

LESSON FOUR

Objectives
1. To review main ideas, events, and vocabulary of reading Assignment #2
2. To preview study questions and vocabulary for Assignment #3
3. To read Assignment #3
4. To evaluate students' oral reading

Activity #1
   Have students answer the study guide questions for Assignment #2 as previously directed. Preview the study questions for Assignment #3 while students have their study questions out.

Activity #2
   Review the vocabulary answers from the reading. Make sure students write down the correct answers. Do the vocabulary worksheet for Assignment #3 orally after you review the worksheet for Assignment #2

Activity #3
   Have students read Assignment #3 of *Fever 1793* out loud in class. You probably know the best way to get readers with your class; pick students at random, ask for volunteers, or use whatever method works best for your group. If you have not yet completed an oral reading evaluation for your students, this would be a good opportunity to do so. A form is included with this unit for your convenience.

ORAL READING EVALUATION *Fever 1793*

Name _____ Class___ Date _____

SKILL	EXCELLENT	GOOD	AVERAGE	FAIR	POOR
Fluency	5	4	3	2	1
Clarity	5	4	3	2	1
Audibility	5	4	3	2	1
Pronunciation	5	4	3	2	1
_____	5	4	3	2	1
_____	5	4	3	2	1

Total _____ Grade _____

Comments:

LESSON FIVE

<u>Objectives</u>
1. To allow students to express personal opinions, using a topic Matilda talks about throughout the novel
2. To evaluate students' writing
3. To tie the book to students' own lives
4. To have students seriously consider their own future plans

<u>Activity #1</u>
   In *Fever 1793*, Matilda dreams of traveling to France then returning to Philadelphia to open her own business. In this essay, students will write about their own dreams after graduation from high school. Distribute Writing Assignment #1 and use the attached rubric to give feedback to your students.

WRITING ASSIGNMENT #1 - *Fever 1793*
Writing to express personal opinions

PROMPT
Matilda dreams of traveling to France where she will bring back fabric, combs, and jewelry that everyone will want to buy from her dry goods store. She then wants to expand her business to include a restaurant, apothecary, school, and hatter's shop, allowing her to own a whole block of businesses. Your assignment is to write about *your* dreams in life.

PREWRITING
Think about all the things you want to do with your life. Be sure to think about your plans after graduation from high school, your choice of career, family expectations, travel, lifestyle, etc. Make a list of all the things you want to do in your life. Remember, your dreams should be specific and cover more than one aspect of your life.

DRAFTING
This essay should be written in first person. It will have an introductory paragraph where you will want to give a vague outline of your dreams.

The body of your essay should include several paragraphs explaining all the details of your dreams for your life. Try to separate your dreams into different categories. Each new aspect of your dream should be a separate body paragraph. Remember to include specific details about your dream like Matilda does in the novel.

Your essay should have a conclusion that wraps up your dreams in life. This could include how you plan on achieving your dreams or how you would feel if you could accomplish all you have dreamed about.

PROMPT
When you finish the rough draft of your composition, ask a student who sits near you to read it. After reading your rough draft, he/she should tell you what he/she liked best about your work, which parts were difficult to understand, and ways in which your work could be improved. Reread your paper considering your critic's comments, and make the corrections you think are necessary. Ask your classmate what he/she thought of each of the characters/events you chose for your assignment.

PROOFREADING
Do a final proofreading of your paper double-checking your grammar, spelling, organization, and the clarity of your ideas.

WRITING EVALUATION FORM - *Fever 1793*

Name _____ Date _____

Writing Assignment # _____   Grade _____

Circle One For Each Item:

Introduction:	excellent	good	fair	poor
Body Paragraphs:	excellent	good	fair	poor
Conclusion:	excellent	good	fair	poor
Grammar:	excellent	good	fair	poor
Spelling:	excellent	good	fair	poor
Punctuation:	excellent	good	fair	poor
Legibility:	excellent	good	fair	poor
_____	excellent	good	fair	poor
_____	excellent	good	fair	poor

Strengths:

Weaknesses:

Comments/Suggestions:

LESSON SIX

Objectives
1. To review main ideas, events, and vocabulary from Assignment #3
2. To help students understand the various ways people deal with troublesome times
3. To allow students to create their own drawing that represent a memory they hold dear to them

Activity #1

Have students answer the study guide questions for Assignment #3 as previously directed.

Activity #2

Review the vocabulary answers from the reading. Make sure students write down the correct answers.

Activity #3

Begin a class discussion on how people are able to cope with difficult times. Ask students how they have dealt with deaths of friends or family members, times of hardship, and other life-altering situations.

Transition your class discussion to talk about how Matilda deals with the many difficult times she faces. Have students give specific examples of problems Matilda has faced and how she has tried to deal with them. Students should point out that Matilda tried to think of what her mother or grandfather would do in the same situation. Students should also point out that Matilda doesn't allow herself to dwell on her situation and relies on her happy memories to get her through the tough times.

Activity #4

To make a connection with the novel, ask students to think of their happiest memory. Encourage them to try to come up with a memory that could get them through a very difficult time, like Matilda does when she is coping with the epidemic of yellow fever. Give students construction paper and markers and have them draw a picture of their favorite, most pleasant memory. Give students an index card and have them write a short paragraph explaining why they cherish that memory and how it could help them in dealing with difficult times. If time permits, allow students to share their work once everyone is finished. You may also want to display students' work in your room.

LESSON SEVEN

Objectives
1. To preview study questions and vocabulary for Assignment #4
2. To have students research and read nonfiction related to the book to help connect the book to real life
3. To broaden students' knowledge about topics related to the book

Activity #1

Take students to the library or media center. With students, brainstorm a list of non-fiction topics that could be related to *Fever 1793*. A short list to get you started is included below.
- Yellow fever in today's society
- Symptoms, common medical treatment, and cures for yellow fever
- The rapid spread of yellow fever in the late 1700s
- The Free African Society
- Medical practices in the late 1700s
- Class differences in the late 1700s
- Bush Hill
- Dr. Benjamin Rush
- French medical practices in the late 1700s
- George Washington
- The American Revolution
- Common trades in the late 1700s

Activity #2

Distribute the Nonfiction Assignment Sheet to students. Explain that students should choose a nonfiction topic related to *Fever 1793*. They should read a substantial article related to that topic and complete the Nonfiction Assignment Sheet for that article. Students may use magazines, newspapers, or the Internet as sources.

Activity #3

Bring the class back together and have each student tell what he/she read about.

Note: Compiling the Nonfiction Assignment Sheets into a booklet makes a nice follow-up activity and a handy reference for students.

Activity #4

Prior to your next class meeting, students should preview the study questions, do the vocabulary worksheet, and read Assignment #4. If students finish their non-fiction assignment early, they may begin working on this assignment in class.

NONFICTION ASSIGNMENT SHEET
(To be completed after reading the required nonfiction article)

Name _____ Date _____

Title of Nonfiction Read _____

Written By _____ Publication Date _____

I. Factual Summary: Write a short summary of the piece you read.

II. Vocabulary
   1. With which vocabulary words in the piece did you encounter some degree of difficulty?

   2. How did you resolve your lack of understanding with these words?

III. Interpretation: What was the main point the author wanted you to get from reading his work?

IV. Criticism
   1. With which points of the piece did you agree or find easy to accept? Why?

   2. With which points of the piece did you disagree or find difficult to believe? Why?

V. Personal Response: What do you think about this piece? OR How does this piece influence your ideas?

LESSON EIGHT

Objectives
1. To review main ideas, events, and vocabulary of Assignment #4
2. To connect the themes in *Fever 1793* with a classical piece of literature
3. To broaden students knowledge on plagues that have occurred in other times and places

Activity #1
Have students answer the study guide questions for Assignment #4 as previously directed.

Activity #2
Review the vocabulary answers from Assignment #4. Make sure students write down the correct answers.

Activity #3
Inform students that several plagues and epidemics have taken place throughout history in various regions of the world. Tell them that several authors before Laurie Halse Anderson wrote on the same topic and themes as she did. Distribute copies of "The Masque of the Red Death" by Edgar Allen Poe and tell students that this story is also about a plague. Let students know that the wealthy, privileged class of people in this society felt they could escape the dangers of the plague like so many tried to in *Fever 1793*.

Note: This is a difficult text for many students. You may want to read it out loud in the classroom, stopping frequently for comprehension checks. If class time allows, you may want to spend additional time on the story. This story should take two days of class time to read and discuss. A copy of the story is available at http://www.online-literature.com/poe/36/

LESSON NINE

Objectives
1. To finish reading "The Masque of the Red Death"
2. To allow students to make connections between Poe's short story and *Fever 1793*
3. To begin exploring some of the themes in *Fever 1793*
4. To preview study questions and vocabulary for Assignment #5
5. To begin reading Assignment #5

Activity #1

Conduct a short review to refresh students on where they left off in their reading of "The Masque of the Red Death." Ask a few comprehension questions and then finish reading the short story together as a class.

Activity #2

Once you have finished the story, hold a class discussion about the theme's Poe wrote about. Prompt students to talk about the symbolism he used throughout the short story as well. Next, ask students to think about the symbolism and themes in *Fever 1793*. Encourage students to point out similarities and differences between the two stories.

Activity #3

Hand out the attached Venn Diagram. Have students label one circle "The Masque of the Red Death" and the other *Fever 1793*. Ask students to write down the differences of the two stories in the corresponding circles, and write down the similarities of the two stories in the overlapping circle. Instruct students to use specific details from the stories to support their answers. Collect diagrams for grading if so desired.

Activity #4

When students finish their Venn Diagrams, they should look ahead at the study questions and do the vocabulary for Assignment #5. Tell students that they also should read Assignment #5 prior to the next class period. Give them the remainder of this class (if time remains) to work on this assignment.

LESSON TEN

Objectives
1. To review main ideas, events, and vocabulary of Assignment #5
2. To help students understand the differences in socioeconomic divisions
3. To help students make connections with the class differences discussed in the novel
4. To preview study questions and vocabulary for Assignment #6

Activity #1
Have students answer the study guide questions for Assignment #5 as previously directed. Preview the questions for Assignment #6 while students have their guides out.

Activity #2
Review the vocabulary answers from Assignment #5. Make sure students write down the correct answers.

Activity #3
Have three different covered tables set up in your classroom. On one table, have something that students really like to eat, such as pizza, small sandwiches, donuts, etc. On another table have something that is just ok in students' minds, like dry cereal, pretzels, etc. On the third table, have food that most students would not like to eat, like pieces of lettuce, plain spaghetti noodles, etc. Make sure theses tables are set up in separate areas of the room and are covered when students enter the room. In a small bag, place slips of paper with the numbers 1, 2, or 3. One will represent the upper class. Be sure to put the fewest number of these slips into the bag. Two will represent the middle class and three will represent the lower class.

Once students have finished the study questions and vocabulary activities, allow them to each pick a slip of paper from the bag. As students are picking a slip of paper from the bag, uncover the food tables and allow students to see the arrangement of the room. Send the students with number ones to the best table, students with number twos to the middle table, and students with number threes to the worst table. Allow students to put food on their plates from their table only and return to their seats.

Once students have begun eating their food, begin a class discussion about how students are feeling about the activity that just took place. Ask the students with food items such as pizza how they are feeling. Ask them if they feel bad that their friends with number threes are picking at lettuce. Ask students with number threes how they feel about people with ones and twos. Ask students with number twos how they feel about their food.

Once you have an open discussion going, connect the activity to social standing and wealth. Explain that those with a number one would have been equal to the Ogilvie family and others that fled to the country where there was plenty of food. Explain that the twos would have been equal to Matilda's family, who had the ability to stay somewhat healthy and had some food to get by, but were still hurt by the epidemic. Explain that the people with threes would have been Eliza or Joseph, people with no ability to leave the city, stuck adding sawdust to their bread to make the flour last longer. Next, point out that those in the number one category would have remained fairly healthy, those in the two category would have about half sick with yellow fever, and those in the third category would have more than half sick and dead.

Conduct a class discussion about how their feelings about those with other numbers are similar to the feelings of people in Philadelphia. Try to point out that those with the really good food are happy, and though they may feel bad for their friends with the worst food, they still don't want to give up what they have or share. Point out that people with the mediocre food are probably somewhat envious but still thankful to have something better than the worst. Get a discussion going about the different perspectives people in different classes in the novel had.

Activity #4

Once students have discussed their feelings about the activity, heard the feelings of others, and made connections with the activity to the feelings of the characters in the novel, instruct students to write a short response about that activity that day. Have them write one paragraph about how they felt during the activity and another paragraph about how they would have felt in their corresponding place in Matilda's society. Allow time for volunteers to share their responses with the class.

Activity #5

Tell students that they should do the vocabulary worksheet for and read Assignment #6 prior to the next class period. Give them the remainder of this class (if time remains) to work on this assignment.

LESSON ELEVEN

Objectives
1. To review main ideas, events, and vocabulary of Assignment #6
2. To give students the opportunity to practice writing to inform
3. To improve students' overall writing ability

Activity #1
Have students answer the study guide questions for Assignment #6 as previously directed.

Activity #2
Review the vocabulary answers from the reading. Make sure students write down the correct answers.

Activity #3
Distribute the RAFT writing assignment to students. Explain that the purpose of this assignment is to write to inform. Tell students that they should select one of the scenarios listed for their second writing assignment. Explain that the "R" stands for the role they will take, or the point of view they are writing from; the "A" stands for the audience they are writing to; the "F" stands for the format of their writing; and the "T" stands for the topic or task. Quickly go over the different scenarios available to them and give the remaining time for students to complete the assignment.

Fever 1793 Writing Assignment – RAFT

Directions: Select one of the following writing situations to use as the topic for your essay.

Role *The voice you take on as a writer; this is the perspective you are writing from*	Audience *Who you are writing to; this is the person that will be reading what you write*	Format *The form your writing will take; this is the type of writing you will complete*	Topic/Task *Your purpose for writing; this is the content or reason for your writing*
Dr. Rush	To a close friend	Letter	Talking about the state of Philadelphia and the fever victims; talking also about his role is helping people
Matilda's Mother	Matilda	Speech	Telling her daughter how proud she is of all she overcame and accomplished
Nell	Herself	Journal Entry	Describing her life while her mother was sick and her life since finding Matilda
Woman in charge of orphanage	Mayor/Town Officials	Newspaper Article	Talking about the state of the orphanage; what needs to be done
Reverend Allen, organizer of the Free African Society	Community of Philadelphia	Speech	Discussing the role the Free African Society played during the epidemic; talking about why his society chose to help; react to how that help was viewed
Mrs. Flagg from Bush Hill	President George Washington	Letter	Describing the change in Bush Hill since Stephen Girard took over; best treatments for the fever; update on status at Bush Hill

WRITING ASSIGNMENT #2 – *Fever 1793*
Writing to inform

PROMPT
Select one of the scenarios listed on the RAFT writing assignment for the topic of your essay. The role is the point of view you are writing from, the audience is who you are writing to, the format is the type of writing you are doing, and the topic/task is the actual information you are writing about.

PREWRITING
Once you have selected your writing scenario, begin to brainstorm ideas. Remember to think about the role you are writing from and the topic you are writing about. Use your book, notes from class, answers from study questions, and notes from the nonfiction articles to help you with your support.

DRAFTING
Write an introductory paragraph that allows the reader to know the role you have assumed and the audience you are writing to. Give a general overview of the points you will make in the body paragraphs of your writing. Use the format of your writing to guide you on how to begin (speech would begin with a little about yourself, letter begins with Dear _____, etc).

In the body paragraphs, give the details of your topic. Use information from the novel, the speaker, and the nonfiction article you read to help provide support. Be sure to reread the topic/task you are writing on and be sure to cover all portions listed there.

In your conclusion paragraph, summarize your main points and conclude the writing assignment. For unity with your writing, you may want to tie in your role and audience once again.

PROMPT
When you finish the rough draft of your composition, ask a student who sits near you to read it. After reading your rough draft, he/she should tell you what he/she liked best about your work, which parts were difficult to understand, and ways in which your work could be improved. Reread your paper considering your critic's comments, and make the corrections you think are necessary. Ask your classmate what he/she thought of each of the characters/events you chose for your assignment.

PROOFREADING
Do a final proofreading of your paper double-checking your grammar, spelling, organization, and the clarity of your ideas.

WRITING EVALUATION FORM - *Fever 1793*

Name _____ Date _____

Writing Assignment # _____   Grade _____

Circle One For Each Item:

Introduction:	excellent	good	fair	poor
Body Paragraphs:	excellent	good	fair	poor
Conclusion:	excellent	good	fair	poor
Grammar:	excellent	good	fair	poor
Spelling:	excellent	good	fair	poor
Punctuation:	excellent	good	fair	poor
Legibility:	excellent	good	fair	poor
Quality of information	excellent	good	fair	poor
_____	excellent	good	fair	poor

Strengths:

Weaknesses:

Comments/Suggestions:

LESSON TWELVE

Objectives
1. To get students thinking about Matilda's character
2. To make students see the importance of strength and weakness in a character
3. To help students connect with the main character of the novel

Activity #1
Note: For this assignment you will need construction paper on a bulletin board and markers.
Begin class by talking about the strengths and weakness of character. Talk about how a person's strengths and weakness make up who they are and are essential to molding who they will become. Connect this discussion with Matilda. Talk briefly about her strengths and weakness in character. Ask students to talk about how those strengths and weaknesses affected Matilda's decisions as she matured over the course of the novel.

After your discussion, have each student choose a partner. The two partners should brainstorm a word or phrase that is one of Matilda's strengths or weaknesses AND a graphic (picture, drawing) that would illustrate their word or phrase as it relates to Matilda. After giving the pairs about 5-10 minutes to come up with a good idea, invite the pairs to go to the bulletin board to write their words/phrases and illustrate them. Students should be able to explain the choices they have made.

Activity #2
Ask students to think about the words, phrases, and pictures they chose. Prompt them to think about personality traits they share with Matilda. Tell students to write a short reflection where they compare and contrast their personalities and characters with Matilda's.

LESSON THIRTEEN

<u>Objectives</u>
1. To bridge a connection between the tragedy that struck in the book to tragedies that occur now
2. To help students see how people react to tragedies and grow as individuals
3. To raise awareness about tragic events that have struck communities recently

<u>Activity #1</u>

Begin class by asking students to think about something that happened in their lives that was really hard for them to overcome. Have them generate a list of tragic or difficult events in their own lives. Next, ask students to write a short response about how they dealt with each of those events. Ask them to write about how dealing with that event helped them grow and learn as an individual. Allow class time for students to share their tragic event and how it changed their lives. (Note: As the teacher, you may want to break the ice by sharing something from your own life and then lead in to the students sharing)

<u>Activity #2</u>

Transition the previous discussion to *Fever 1793*. Ask students to talk about how the city of Philadelphia reacted to the sudden outbreak of yellow fever. Generate a list of varying ways the people in the community dealt with this tragedy. Next, create a list of ways people responded to help. Give students some time to discuss how they would have reacted if they were in Matilda's situation. Try to point out to students that those who helped (people at Bush Hill, members of the Free African Society, volunteers at orphanages) grew as individuals. Prompt your students to discuss Matilda's growth by dealing with the tragedy when it struck her family, and how she grew even more once she volunteered to help out.

After students have had time to discuss Matilda's growth, instruct them to create a time line of events in her life from before the fever broke out through the end of the novel. Ask students to only place events on the time line that had a significant impact on Matilda's life and growth from a child to an adult.

Once students have completed their time lines, come together as a class to discuss the specific events that were included on students' individual time lines. Ask students to explain why they included each event and how they impacted Matilda's growth as an individual.

Note: To prepare for this next discussion, you may want to go online and print some photographs to share with your students from recent tragedies (hurricane Katrina, the World Trade Center attack, the tsunami, genocide in African countries, etc). You may also want to include statistics such as the death toll, the various ways different humanitarian groups helped, how individuals raised money and sent supplies, etc.

Activity #3
Once you have bridged a connection with personal growth in dealing with a tragedy between students' personal lives and Matilda, try to bridge a connection with modern tragedies. Tell students that over the next few days they will be learning about modern tragedies in the world, and that they too will have the chance to grow as an individual and participate in helping just as Matilda does in *Fever 1793*.

Ask your students to brainstorm a list of local, national, and international tragedies that have occurred within the past 10 years. Ask students to think about how people in those communities responded to the tragedy. Generate a list for each tragedy about how people in neighboring communities have helped out. Try to talk about the overall growth of the community as well as the individuals that helped out.

LESSON FOURTEEN

Objectives
1. To bring ideas from the book into real life
2. To inform students about tragedies that occur now and how to become involved
3. To try to inspire an interest in helping as Matilda does in the book, leading to growth and awareness

Activity #1
We have set this day aside for a guest speaker. Invite one or more of the following people from your community to speak to your class:

- Someone who has been through a large-scale tragedy (survivor of World Trade Center attacks, hurricane victim, etc)
- People from various humanitarian groups that organize aid when needed (someone from your local ONE chapter, Red Cross, etc)

Divide your class time according to how many speakers you're able to acquire. Remember to allow time for students to ask questions. Let each speaker know how much time he/she will have for the presentation. Allow for time at the end of the class for students to make connections with what they have learned from the speakers with what they have read in *Fever 1793*.

Follow Up: Be sure you and your students write thank you notes to each of your guests. At the very least, get a thank you card for each guest and have each of your students sign it (with any personal responses, if there is room).

LESSON FIFTEEN

Objectives
1. To bring ideas from the book into real life
2. To inform students about tragedies that occur now and how to become involved
3. To try to inspire an interest in helping as Matilda does in the book, leading to growth and awareness

Activity #1

Have the following quote from chapter 15 of *Fever 1793* written on the board: "Have you considered what you might do to help? You are young and strong. We have a real need for you."

Ask students if they have ever thought about what they might to do help others in need. Allow students to share experiences they or their families have had in helping someone out. Next, explain that there is a real need for help in places all over the world. Tell students that many people in poor countries still suffer and die from yellow fever and malaria (a closely related disease), even though there is a simple vaccine to cure both. Explain that there are people who are living in poverty with no food and surrounded by disease, and that there are several organizations that allow ways for students to help.

Activity #2

Take your students to the computer lab. Divide students into groups of two or three and have them sit at a computer work station together. Tell your students that they will be researching different humanitarian groups and working to inform others about this campaign. Each of the sites listed below have several videos to educate students on the current situation, ways to get involved, and statistics to help spread awareness about what is happening in other places. You can assign each group of students to research one of the three sites listed below, add additional sites you are aware of, or have the class select just one organization to research. Instruct students to watch the available videos and browse the site they are assigned. Hand out the attached form to direct students in their research. Popular humanitarian groups are listed below:

- ONE (available at www.one.org): An organization committed to fighting poverty and the spread of disease in Africa. Includes several celebrity endorsements such as Brad Pitt, Tom Hanks, Pat Robertson, Kate Hudson, Jamie Foxx, Penelope Cruz, Dave Matthews, Salma Hayek, George Clooney, Bill Gates, and many, many others.

- Nothing but Nets (available at www.nothingbutnets.org): An organization that distributes mosquito netting in countries where malaria and other deadly diseases spread by mosquitoes kill thousands each year.

- The International Rescue Committee (available at www.theirc.org): An organization that provides aid, assistance, safety, and relocation for those who have been victims of violence or oppression. Not On Our Watch (a group founded by the leading men of the Ocean 11, 12, and 13 movies–Brad Pitt, Matt Damon, George Clooney, Don Cheadle, and Jerry Weintraub) has recently partnered with the International Rescue Committee with information about that campaign on the IRC site as well.

Activity #3
Once students have finished conducting their research, bring the class back together to discuss what they have learned. If possible, create a chart on the board and allow students from each group to add information about the humanitarian organization they researched. Talk to the class about getting involved in an organization and giving back to society just as Matilda does in the novel. Explain that helping out will add to personal growth as well.

Activity #4
Allow students to select a humanitarian group to get involved with. Put students into groups according the organization they are most interested in working with. Give students time to plan ways they can raise awareness around the school and how they can help out. Instruct each group to come up with two or three poster ideas, a catchy announcement for the morning show, and a way to raise money around school. Students should spend some time at home developing these ideas as well and will have time to meet as a group in a later lesson.

Humanitarian Group Research

What is the name of the organization you are researching?

What does the organization do?

Why is the work the organization is doing important?

Who is involved with the organization (famous people, founders, etc)?

What are the advertising campaigns and slogans for this organization?

What are three ways you can participate in this organization?

    1.

    2.

    3.

List five facts or statistics about the problem that would be surprising to someone not involved:

    1.

    2.

    3.

    4.

    5.

What work has the organization done in the past? What is their current progress like?

LESSON SIXTEEN

<u>Objectives</u>
1. To give students the opportunity to practice writing to persuade
2. To improve students' overall writing ability
3. To connect ideas and facts learned from the book and additional activities with a real-life situation

<u>Activity #1</u>
In the previous lessons, students learned about the importance of helping others and the growth it can spark within an individual. In this writing assignment, students will write to persuade someone to participate in one of the humanitarian organizations they researched in a previous lesson. Distribute Writing Assignment 3 to students and give them the remaining class time to write.

<u>Note</u>: As students complete this writing assignment, call individuals up for writing conferences on the past two writing assignments. Use the evaluation form to guide in your conference.

WRITING ASSIGNMENT #3 – *Fever 1793*
Writing to Persuade

PROMPT
Matilda works with members of the Free African Society to care for victims of the yellow fever. She also adopts Nell, an orphan from yellow fever, and cares for her. In the previous lessons you have learned about the importance of helping others and the growth it can bring to an individual. Your assignment is to write a persuasive essay, convincing others in your community or school to get involved with a humanitarian organization.

PREWRITING
Think about the various organizations you studied with your class. Review your notes containing the importance of these organizations, what they do, and why they are important. Formulate a list of reasons why people should help out with your chosen organization.

DRAFTING
Write an introductory paragraph that introduces the reader to the organization you are persuading them to participate in. Give some general information about the humanitarian organization and the reasons why others should get involved. Be sure to give a general overview of the points you will make in the body paragraphs of your writing.

In the body paragraphs, give specific details about what your organization does and why it is important. You may want to refer to others who are involved, the specific work the organization does, and the factual information to backup why the work is necessary. You will also want to mention the personal reasons why people should get involved. Remember, each time you make a new point, begin a new paragraph.

In your conclusion paragraph, summarize your main points and conclude the writing assignment. Try to end with a powerful statement that will help readers better understand why they should participate in the organization you are recommending.

PROMPT
When you finish the rough draft of your composition, ask a student who sits near you to read it. After reading your rough draft, he/she should tell you what he/she liked best about your work, which parts were difficult to understand, and ways in which your work could be improved. Reread your paper considering your critic's comments, and make the corrections you think are necessary. Ask your classmate what he/she thought of each of the characters/events you chose for your assignment.

PROOFREADING
Do a final proofreading of your paper double-checking your grammar, spelling, organization, and the clarity of your ideas.

WRITING EVALUATION FORM - *Fever 1793*

Name _____ Date _____

Writing Assignment # _____   Grade _____

Circle One For Each Item:

Introduction:	excellent	good	fair	poor
Body Paragraphs:	excellent	good	fair	poor
Conclusion:	excellent	good	fair	poor
Grammar:	excellent	good	fair	poor
Spelling:	excellent	good	fair	poor
Punctuation:	excellent	good	fair	poor
Legibility:	excellent	good	fair	poor
Persuasiveness:	excellent	good	fair	poor
_____	excellent	good	fair	poor

Strengths:

Weaknesses:

Comments/Suggestions:

LESSON SEVENTEEN

Objectives
1. To bring ideas from the book into real life
2. To inform students about tragedies that occur now and how to become involved
3. To try to inspire an interest in helping as Matilda does in the book, leading to growth and awareness
4. To discuss the novel on a deeper than direct-recall level
5. To prepare students for questions and topics covered on the test
6. To allow students to make personal connection with the text

Activity #1

Place your students into the groups they were previously working in (groups by humanitarian organization). Students should already have their ideas for posters, school announcement programs, and ways to raise money and awareness for the organization on a school-wide level. Give students posterboard and markers and allow them this time to create their posters to raise awareness and get other students involved in their chosen organization. You may want to suggest they use celebrity endorsements, catchy slogans, shocking statistics, and colorful graphics. If students finish their posters, have them work with you to get the announcement they want on the school morning show and review their plan to raise money.

Note: You may need to check with the principal and other teachers before hanging posters and beginning to raise money/supplies in your school to be sure there are no conflicts.

Activity #2

Choose the questions from the Extra Discussion Questions/Writing Assignments which seem most appropriate for your students. A class discussion of these questions is most effective if students have been given the opportunity to formulate answers to the questions prior to the discussion. To this end, you may either have all the students formulate answers to all the questions, divide your class into groups and assign one or more questions to each group, or you could assign one question to each student in your class. The option you choose will make a difference in the amount of class time needed for this activity.

Note: The use of graphic organizers may be helpful to students in preparing their answers. Encourage them to use any diagrams or graphics that they feel are necessary.

EXTRA DISCUSSION QUESTIONS/WRITING ASSIGNMENTS
Fever 1793

Interpretive
1. From what point of view is the story told, and why is that important?

2. What is the setting, and what does it add to the story?

3. What are the main conflicts in the story? Describe each fully.

4. Describe the author's writing style. Give specific examples to support your ideas.

5. How does the author use quotes from famous people in the novel? What does this add to the story?

6. List five of Matilda's most important character traits and give examples of each.

7. Describe the relationship that Matilda and Nathaniel have.

Critical
8. Matilda wants to go to Polly's funeral but her mother says no. Her mother claims it will give her nightmares; however Matilda doesn't believe it. What is the real reason Matilda's mother refuses to let her attend Polly's funeral?

9. How has Matilda's mother changed since the death of her husband?

10. Matilda's grandfather says, "Some days I'd rather face the British again than listen to the sound of my dear daughter-in-law." What does this say about the character of Matilda's mother? Why does she act the way she does?

11. Matilda says, "I had plenty of ideas about running the coffeehouse, all of them different from Mother's." What is her vision for the coffeehouse? Why does it differ so much from the vision her mother holds?

12. Compare and contrast the way Matilda's mother feels about the possibility of a fever spreading with the way her grandfather feels. Who does Matilda side with? Why do you think that is?

13. Matilda's mother says, "It's not too early to search for a suitable man. With your manners, it could take years." How does Matilda's mother's plan for her future differ from the one Matilda envisions?

14. When Matilda's mother falls ill, her family uses a doctor whose "hands were uncommonly dirty, and he smelled of rum." Why does Matilda's grandfather ask a doctor of this sort to treat her mother?

Fever 1793 Extra Discussion Questions, Page 2

15. Mr. Rowley and Dr. Kerr both treat Matilda's mother. Compare and contrast the way they treat her and their diagnosis of her illness. Why are the two views so different?

16. Matilda is left all alone to care for her mother overnight. Analyze how she felt taking care of her mother all by herself. What thoughts and emotions were running through her?

17. Matilda's mother is yelling at her to leave. However, Matilda thinks, "I had to help her. She was depending on me." Describe how this contrast in wanting to help and being asked to leave affects Matilda emotionally.

18. In chapter 14 Matilda has a unique dream. Review the details of the dream. What does this dream mean?

19. Why are the doctors at Bush Hill able to cure yellow fever victims, while other doctors are unable to save anyone from dying?

20. Matilda asks how many people have died since she and her grandfather fled the city. The man they are traveling with reports several thousand have died and says, "It slowed down those few cool days, but as soon as the temperature rose again, so did the number of corpses." What does the temperature have to do with the spread of yellow fever?

21. "The second floor looked as I had left it, except that Mother was missing. The powerful stench of sickness lingered." Describe how Matilda feels going back home.

22. "Eliza wouldn't go. She has family here and would have wanted to help. You know Eliza would never run from trouble." Compare and contrast the way Eliza is treated in society because of the color of her skin with the way she treats others in that same society.

23. Compare and contrast the funeral Matilda envisions for her grandfather with the one that is held.

24. Eliza tells Matilda, "You can only climb one mountain at a time." What does she mean by this?

25. "Reverend Allen said this was a chance for black people to show we are every bit as good and important and useful as white people. The Society organizes folks to visits the sick, to care for them and bury them if they died." The black people in Philadelphia are treated so poorly and yet they work for free to care for the white people that mistreated them. What does this say about the character of the white people in this city? What does it say about the character of the black people in this city?

26. Even though it seems like a charitable thing to do, Matilda admits that taking care of Nell is selfish. How is this true?

Fever 1793 Extra Discussion Questions, Page 3

27. Matilda has trouble coping with her emotions as she helps Eliza with the yellow fever victims, even though she has experienced the same thing while at Bush Hill. Why is this experience so much harder for her?

28. "Though we were all healed of the fever, some wounds were inside the heart and would mend slowly." What does Matilda mean by this?

29. Throughout the novel Matilda has felt that she was more of a bother and disappointment to her mother than someone her mother could love and be proud of. How does the reader know that Matilda's outlook on how her mother feels about her is not true?

30. At the beginning of the novel Matilda is a teenager, and yet at the end she is a successful businesswoman. Trace Matilda's progress in moving from childhood to adulthood over the course of the novel.

31. How is the color yellow a symbol in the story?

Critical/Personal Response

32. The elite people in society blame the spread of illness on the lower class. The wealthy are also able to travel away from the city to avoid sickness. What does this say about the class differences in society? Give an example of class differences in present society.

33. "I don't believe it…people exaggerate," says Matilda's grandfather. Despite all the evidence of yellow fever, many people still refuse to believe that is the cause of the recent deaths. Why do so many people, including Matilda's grandfather, choose not to see the truth?

34. Yellow fever is spreading quickly throughout the city. Formulate two reasons as to how the disease might be spreading so quickly.

35. "I waited for his advice. It did not come. That scared me more than anything. He was waiting for me to decide what to do." Matilda complains when she is treated like a child, but when she is given responsibility she is frightened. Why is this?

36. Matilda's mom is constantly harping on her about her attitude. Her mother likes to talk about how life was when she was a kid, reminding Matilda that kids these days have grown lazier and pay less attention to acting the way they should. Do parents in this time period still feel the same way about their children? Have your parents ever compared you to how they were as a child?

37. Matilda's mother works very hard to keep up appearances in front on Mrs. Ogilvie. Why does she try so hard to fit in with people of her stature in society? Describe a time in your life when you tried hard to fit in with a particular group of people.

Fever 1793 Extra Discussion Questions, Page 4

38. Matilda depicts her mother's illness with great detail. She talks about her yellow eyes, the blood in her vomit, her violent convulsions, and foul-smelling black liquid coming out of her body. She also describes how helpless she feels and how desperately she wants to help her mother get better. As a reader, what was going through your mind when Matilda was watching her mother creep closer to death?

39. Eliza stays in the city to take care of Matilda's mother. She says to Matilda, "Hush, child. I'm doing no more than your mother would do in my place. This is how the Lord wants us to treat each other." Do you think Matilda's mother would stay behind to care for Eliza if she were sick?

39. Matilda fears that she will lose her grandfather to yellow fever after they have been abandoned on the country road. How do you think she is feeling? What would you have done in this situation?

41. When Matilda and her grandfather are left on the side of the road they ask, "Have you no mercy?" The men turn away and leave, offering no help. Do you think the men were right in refusing to help Matilda's grandfather? Explain your answer.

42. Matilda is optimistic that though there has been no word from her mother, everything is fine. Do you think it is healthy for her to remain so positive? Explain your answer.

43. Matilda thinks of herself as an adult and gets angry when people treat her like a child. However, when Matilda is asked to help care for fever victims and orphaned children, she claims she can't help because she is too young. Matilda then thinks, "The first time anyone treats me like a woman and I respond like an infant." How are the teenage years a difficult time for Matilda? Describe her struggle between wanting to be an adult, and still feeling like a child. Do you ever feel this way? Explain your answer.

44. Matilda is cured from yellow fever by kind individuals at Bush Hill who risked their own lives to care for the sick. Once Matilda is discharged, they ask her what she will do to help. Matilda has no interest in helping and just wants to find her mother and get back to the life she used to live. After receiving free care from the people at Bush Hill, do you think Matilda should do something to help? What would you do in her situation?

45. Matilda says, "Hundreds of people swarmed to town. The returnees were all well-fed. They called to each other in annoying, bright voices. I wanted to tell them to hush. It felt like they were dancing on a grave with no thought to the suffering they had escaped." How is Matilda feeling about the stark contrast between the wealthy who escaped the fever and the poor who suffered miserably? Do you think the wealthy people should be acting the way they are? Do you think economic disparity is present in society today? Explain your answer.

Fever 1793 Extra Discussion Questions, Page 5

46. When Matilda decides to make Eliza a partner, Joseph suggests they make it official with a lawyer. He says, "Some folk will say Eliza took advantage of you. They don't like to see black people move up." Is it right that the black people are still treated like second-rate citizens after all the work the black community did to care for the white people with yellow fever? How would you feel if you lived back then? Do you think racism is still a problem in society today? Explain your answer.

Personal Response

47. Matilda is upset at her mother for not allowing her to attend Polly's funeral. She yells, "Why are you so horrid?" at her mother, but a second later thinks, "As soon as the angry words were out of my mouth, I knew I had gone too far." Give an example of when you have said something out of anger that you later regretted. How did that event shape the way you argued in the future?

48. "It's hard to believe it's over…It feels so strange, so sudden. We're supposed to go back to the way we lived before, but everything has changed." How do people recover and get back to life as usual after a tragic event?

49. Matilda says, "Daughters aren't supposed to bathe their mothers." The role of mother and daughter are reversed once Matilda's mother gets sick. Describe a time in your life when you felt the role of parent and child were reversed in your life. How did that time make you feel?

50. Matilda's grandfather talks about his role in the War of Independence and the contributions his generation made to the freedom of America from Great Britain. Matilda's mother talks about how when she was a child she was always up early and tending to her chores before anyone had to ask, never once complaining. The idea that older generations think they behaved better and contributed more to society is not a new one. Do you see this same mind-set in society today? Do you think this will always be how the older generation thinks? Explain your answer.

51. People in the coffeehouse talk about the recent deaths of people in the community. A doctor comments that the yellow fever may be the cause. Someone else says, "You doctors are all alike, scaring us to earn more business." Do people want to know the truth or do they wish to remain ignorant about what is happening in the city? Support your answer with reasoning why people feel that way.

52. Matilda says, "There were so many things she had tried to teach me, but I didn't listen." What is something your parents have tried to teach you that you never paid attention to?

Fever 1793 Extra Discussion Questions, Page 6

53. Matilda is forced to leave her sick mother behind and travel with her grandfather to the country for safety. Would you be able to leave someone in your family behind in that situation?

54. Matilda wakes up and says, "My sheets and shift were soaked through with sweat, blood, and the foul-smelling black substance that marked a victim of yellow fever." What would you do if you awoke in a strange place and saw that you had all the symptoms of a deadly disease? What would be going through your mind?

55. "I shook my head mutely. No. No. This would not happen. No. Please God. Anything but this…I covered my mouth to hold in the scream and rocked back and forth…Don't die. I couldn't hold the words back…Please don't die. I love you. Please, please. Oh dead God, please don't die." What would you do if you were Matilda and all alone in the world?

56. "What did it feel like to die? Was it a peaceful sleep? Some thought it was full of either trumpet-blowing angels or angry devils." What do you think death is like?

57. "I didn't have time to dream or plan. I would deal with each hour as it came, one step at a time." Matilda has been forced to face the harsh realities of the world she is living in. Describe a time in your life when you had to abandon your dreams and face the realities of a serious problem.

58. Matilda isn't sure what to do with her life. The fever is finally over, yet she has not heard from her mother. If you were Matilda's friend, what advice would you give her?

QUOTATIONS - *Fever 1793*

1. "Black people were treated differently than white people; that was plain to see, but Eliza said nobody could tell her what to do or where to go, and no one would ever, ever beat her again." Chapter 2

2. "My father had only been dead two years, so Mother knew just what lay in Eliza's heart. They both supped sorrow with a big spoon." Chapter 2

3. "I don't need a husband to run the coffeehouse, Mother. You don't have one." Chapter 6

4. "Me who stood unafraid before British cannon run in fear from this foul pestilence. I fear for Philadelphia. I fear for the people, I fear for myself." Chapter 8

5. "There were so many things she had tried to teach me, but I didn't listen. I leaned over to kiss her forehead. A tear slipped out before I could stop it." Chapter 9

6. "There could be no running from this. Hiding from death was not like hiding from Mother when she wanted me to scrub kettles, or ignoring Silas when he begged for food." Chapter 20

7. "I glanced at Eliza. 'May I go?' 'You don't need my permission,' Eliza said. She was right. I could choose for myself." Chapter 26

8. "It's hard to believe it's over…It feels so strange, so sudden. We're supposed to go back to the way we lived before, but everything has changed." Chapter 26

9. "Though we were all healed of the fever, some wounds were inside the heart and would mend slowly." Chapter 27

10. "Looking down the peaceful street, it seemed no one could imagine the terror we had all endured…Philadelphia had moved on." Epilogue

LESSON EIGHTEEN

Objectives
1. To bring ideas from the book into real life
2. To inform students about tragedies that occur now and how to become involved
3. To try to inspire an interest in helping as Matilda does in the book, leading to growth and awareness
4. To discuss the novel on a deeper than direct-recall level
5. To prepare students for questions and topics covered on the test
6. To allow students to make personal connection with the text

Activity #1
Complete the Extra Discussion Questions from the previous assignment.

Activity #2
Allow students to work in groups to complete their campaign to raise awareness on the humanitarian organization of their choice. You will need to make sure their posters are hung and that their plan to raise awareness and get involved is appropriate. You will most likely want to devote either the first or last few minutes of class time for the remainder of this unit to check on the progress of collecting money/supplies.

LESSON NINETEEN

Objectives
1. To have students make a personal connection with the text
2. To have students practice writing a letter
3. To have students show the author their appreciation for the book
4. To evaluate students' reaction to the unit

Activity #1
Give students the Letter to the Author assignment sheet. If needed, review how to write a formal letter with your students. Give students most of the class time to write their letter. Once you have proofread all the letters and students have had a chance to correct any errors, mail the letters to Laurie Halse Anderson at:

Laurie Halse Anderson
c/o Penguin Publicity
345 Hudson Street
New York, NY 10014

Activity #2
Give students the *Fever 1793* Unit Reaction sheet. Give them a chance to answer the questions and give feedback about the unit. Read over the feedback and make any necessary adjustments to the unit before you begin to teach it the following year.

Letter to the Author

Often times, books are written to make people think about serious issues. Think about the point the author was trying to make in writing this book. Then, compose a letter to the author expressing how this book has affected your life.

Topics to include in your letter:
- What you liked about the book
- How you could relate to this book
- How realistic the book was
- What you learned from the book
- What issues the book made you think about
- How you felt when reading the book
- How you have changed since reading the book
- Anything else you think the author should know

Necessary Elements:
- You should begin your letter by saying Dear Ms. Anderson:
- You should have an introductory paragraph where you introduce yourself.
- You should have body paragraphs.
- You should have a friendly conclusion to the letter.
- Underneath your signature you should include your home address and email address in case the author wishes to write back to you.

Remember to proofread this letter and turn it in to me free of errors. I will grade your letter, allow you to make any changes that are needed, and then I will mail your letters to the author of your book. Most authors enjoy receiving letters from readers and like to see how their hard work has affected others. Some authors even respond to letters from their readers, so don't be surprised if you get a reply.

Fever 1793 Unit Reaction

1. What were your overall impressions of *Fever 1793*?

2. How likely are you to read one of Laurie Halse Anderson's other books?

3. How likely are you to read other young adult historical fiction novels?

4. What was your favorite assignment in the unit? Why?

5. What was your least favorite assignment in the unit? Why?

6. What was most helpful to you in this unit?

7. What assignment do you think should be changed? Why?

8. What was something that surprised you when doing research on a humanitarian organization?

9. How did you feel about getting involved in helping a humanitarian organization? How did it change you as an individual?

10. How has this book and all of the assignments done with it affected your life (the decisions you make, how you view others, etc)?

Use the space below to write any other comments you have regarding this unit:

LESSON TWENTY

Objective
To review all of the vocabulary work done in this unit

Activity #1:
Choose one (or more) of the vocabulary review activities listed below and spend your class period as directed in the activity. Some of the materials for these review activities are located in the Vocabulary Resource Materials section in this LitPlan.

VOCABULARY REVIEW ACTIVITIES

1. Divide your class into two teams and have an old-fashioned spelling or definition bee.

2. Give each of your students (or students in groups of two, three or four) a *Fever 1793* Vocabulary Word Search Puzzle. The person (group) to find all of the vocabulary words in the puzzle first wins.

3. Give students a *Fever 1793* Vocabulary Word Search Puzzle without the word list. The person or group to find the most vocabulary words in the puzzle wins.

4. Use a *Fever 1793* Vocabulary Crossword Puzzle. Put the puzzle onto a transparency on the overhead projector (so everyone can see it), and do the puzzle together as a class.

5. Give students a *Fever 1793* Vocabulary Matching Worksheet to do.

6. Divide your class into two teams. Use *Fever 1793* vocabulary words with their letters jumbled as a word list. Student 1 from Team A faces off against Student 1 from Team B. You write the first jumbled word on the board. The first student (1A or 1B) to unscramble the word wins the chance for his/her team to score points. If 1A wins the jumble, go to student 2A and give him/her a definition. He/she must give you the correct spelling of the vocabulary word which fits that definition. If he/she does, Team A scores a point, and you give student 3A a definition for which you expect a correctly spelled matching vocabulary word. Continue giving Team A definitions until some team member makes an incorrect response. An incorrect response sends the game back to the jumbled-word face off, this time with students 2A and 2B. Instead of repeating giving definitions to the first few students of each team, continue with the student after the one who gave the last incorrect response on the team. For example, if Team B wins the jumbled-word face-off, and student 5B gave the last incorrect answer for Team B, you would start this round of definition questions with student 6B, and so on. The team with the most points wins!

7. Have students write a story in which they correctly use as many vocabulary words as possible. Have students read their compositions orally! Post the most original compositions on your bulletin board!

LESSON TWENTY-ONE

Objective:
To review the main ideas and events in *Fever 1793*

Activity:
Choose one of the review games/activities suggested in this unit and spend your class time as directed there.

REVIEW GAMES/ACTIVITIES *Fever 1793*

1. Ask the class to make up a unit test for *Fever 1793*. The test should have 4 sections: matching, true/false, short answer, and essay. Students may use 1/2 period to make the test and then swap papers and use the other 1/2 class period to take a test a classmate has devised. (open book) You may want to use the unit test included in this packet or take questions from the students' unit tests to formulate your own test.

2. Take 1/2 period for students to make up true and false questions (including the answers). Collect the papers and divide the class into two teams. Draw a big tic-tac-toe board on the chalk board. Make one team X and one team O. Ask questions to each side, giving each student one turn. If the question is answered correctly, that students' team's letter (X or O) is placed in the box. If the answer is incorrect, no letter is placed in the box. The object is to get three in a row like tic-tac-toe. You may want to keep track of the number of games won for each team.

3. Take 1/2 period for students to make up questions (true/false and short answer). Collect the questions. Divide the class into two teams. You'll alternate asking questions to individual members of teams A & B (like in a spelling bee). The question keeps going from A to B until it is correctly answered, then a new question is asked. A correct answer does not allow the team to get another question. Correct answers are +2 points; incorrect answers are -1 point.

4. Have students pair up and quiz each other from their study guides and class notes.

5. Give students a *Fever 1793* crossword puzzle to complete.

6. Play What's My Line?. This is similar to the old television show. Students assume the roles of different characters from the epic. One student gives clues to the class, or to a panel of contestants. The contestants try to guess the identity of the guest. Students may enjoy assisting you in creating rules and procedures for the game.

Review Games Page 2

7. Divide your class into two teams. Use *Fever 1793* crossword words with their letters jumbled as a word list. Student 1 from Team A faces off against Student 1 from Team B. You write the first jumbled word on the board. The first student (1A or 1B) to unscramble the word wins the chance for his/her team to score points. If 1A wins the jumble, go to student 2A and give him/her a clue. He/she must give you the correct word which matches that clue. If he/she does, Team A scores a point, and you give student 3A a clue for which you expect another correct response. Continue giving Team A clues until some team member makes an incorrect response. An incorrect response sends the game back to the jumbled-word face off, this time with students 2A and 2B. Instead of repeating giving clues to the first few students of each team, continue with the student after the one who gave the last incorrect response on the team. For example, if Team B wins the jumbled-word face-off, and student 5B gave the last incorrect answer for Team B, you would start this round of clue questions with student 6B, and so on. The team with the most points wins!

8. Play Jeopardy. Divide the class into two groups. Assign each group a category or book from the epic and have them devise answers for that category. Play the game according to the television show procedures.

9. Play Drawing in the Details. This is similar to Pictionary. Divide students into teams. A student from one team draws a scene from the epic. (You may want to specify the Book or section.) Drawings should be kept simple, to keep the pace lively. Students in the opposing team locate the scene in their books and read it aloud. If they are incorrect, the illustrator's team has a chance to guess. Involve students in setting up a scoring system and any other necessary rules.

UNIT TESTS

SHORT ANSWER UNIT TEST 1 - *Fever 1793*

I. Matching/Identify

_____ 1. Joseph   A. People who are making money off fever victims

_____ 2. Coffeehouse   B. Family Matilda's mother hopes her daughter can marry into

_____ 3. Mother   C. General Matilda's grandfather served under

_____ 4. Nell   D. Place where Matilda's mother has been

_____ 5. Ogilvie   E. Person that nurses Matilda back to health from the fever

_____ 6. Bush Hill   F. Painter Matilda flirts with

_____ 7. Mrs. Flagg   G. Social gathering spot to talk news and politics

_____ 8. Frost   H. Man whose medical practices harm people more than help

_____ 9. Nathaniel   I. Man who organized help for people stuck in Philadelphia

_____ 10. Eliza   J. Child who lost her mother to the fever and lives with Matilda

_____ 11. Apothecary   K. Man who changed Bush Hill into a safe place

_____ 12. Farm   L. Helps Matilda defend her home from robbers

_____ 13. Bleeding   M. Father of two children; lost his wife to the fever

_____ 14. Rev. Allen   N. Capitol of the United States during this time

_____ 15. Dr. Rush   O. Woman who gives her services to help others in need

_____ 16. Washington   P. Worst way to cure yellow fever

_____ 17. Girard   Q. Widow who owns a respectable coffeehouse

_____ 18. Grandfather   R. Refuses to believe that the disease spreading is yellow fever

_____ 19. Philadelphia S. Place where French doctors work to heal fever victims

_____ 20. Sword   T. Best way to stop the spread of the fever

Fever 1793 Short Answer Unit Test 1 Page 2

II. Short Answer

1. What future does Matilda dream of for herself?

2. Aside from telling the time, why do the church bells ring?

3. Matilda's mother and grandfather have different views regarding the spread of a fever. What does Matilda's mother want to do? What does her grandfather want to do?

4. How do Matilda and her grandfather end up stranded on the side of the road?

5. Why is Matilda terrified to be at Bush Hill?

Fever 1793 Short Answer Unit Test 1 Page 3

6. Describe Philadelphia when Matilda and her grandfather return.

7. Why is it difficult for farmers to come to Philadelphia to sell food?

8. Why is Matilda so against calling a doctor to help William, Robert, and Nell?

9. Why does Matilda need a lawyer to make Eliza a full partner of the coffeehouse?

10. Describe business at the coffeehouse after Matilda takes over.

Fever 1793 Short Answer Unit Test 1 Page 4

IV. Vocabulary

Write down the vocabulary words. Go back later and write down the correct definition for each word.

	Word	Definition
1		
2		
3		
4		
5		
6		
7		
8		
9		
10		

Fever 1793 Short Answer Unit Test 1 Page 5

IV. Essay: Select *one* of the following topics and respond in an essay.

"Eliza wouldn't go. She has family here and would have wanted to help. You know Eliza would never run from trouble." Compare and contrast the way Eliza is treated in society because of the color of her skin with the way she treats others in that same society.

OR

Throughout the novel Matilda has felt that she was more of a bother and disappointment to her mother than someone her mother could love and be proud of. How does the reader know that Matilda's outlook on how her mother feels about her is not true?

SHORT ANSWER UNIT TEST 1 ANSWER KEY - *Fever 1793*

I. Matching/Identify

M	1. Joseph	A.	People who are making money off fever victims
G	2. Coffeehouse	B.	Family Matilda's mother hopes her daughter can marry into
Q	3. Mother	C.	General Matilda's grandfather served under
J	4. Nell	D.	Place where Matilda's mother has been
B	5. Ogilvie	E.	Person that nurses Matilda back to health from the fever
S	6. Bush Hill	F.	Painter Matilda flirts with
E	7. Mrs. Flagg	G.	Social gathering spot to talk news and politics
T	8. Frost	H.	Man whose medical practices harm people more than help
F	9. Nathaniel	I.	Man who organized help for people stuck in Philadelphia
O	10. Eliza	J.	Child who lost her mother to the fever and lives with Matilda
A	11. Apothecary	K.	Man who changed Bush Hill into a safe place
D	12. Farm	L.	Helps Matilda defend her home from robbers
P	13. Bleeding	M.	Father of two children; lost his wife to the fever
I	14. Rev. Allen	N.	Capitol of the United States during this time
H	15. Dr. Rush	O.	Woman who gives her services to help others in need
C	16. Washington	P.	Worst way to cure yellow fever
K	17. Girard	Q.	Widow who owns a respectable coffeehouse
R	18. Grandfather	R.	Refuses to believe that the disease spreading is yellow fever
N	19. Philadelphia	S.	Place where French doctors work to heal fever victims
L	20. Sword	T.	Best way to stop the spread of the fever

Fever 1793 Short Answer Unit Test 1 Answer Key Page 2

II. Short Answer

1. What future does Matilda dream of for herself?
    Matilda dreams of traveling to France to bring back beautiful fabric, combs, and jewelry to sell in her own dry goods store. She also dreams of owning a whole block of other businesses including a restaurant, apothecary, school, and hatter's shop.

2. Aside from telling the time, why do the church bells ring?
    The church bells ring to signify another death in the city. They ring once for each year the person lived.

3. Matilda's mother and grandfather have different views regarding the spread of a fever. What does Matilda's mother want to do? What does her grandfather want to do?
    Matilda's mother wants to flee to the country to avoid getting sick, but Matilda's grandfather doesn't believe the sickness is yellow fever. He wants to keep running the coffeehouse and try to earn a big profit.

4. How do Matilda and her grandfather end up stranded on the side of the road?
    The men on horseback are actually men with a doctor inspecting visitors for signs of yellow fever before they can enter their city. The men see Matilda's grandfather cough violently and assume he is sick. The farmer they are traveling with throws them out of the wagon and leaves with all of their belongings

5. Why is Matilda terrified to be at Bush Hill?
    Matilda has heard that Bush Hill is a dangerous place. She heard that it is not respectable and that dead bodies were piled everywhere while thieves preyed on the weak.

6. Describe Philadelphia when Matilda and her grandfather return.
    Instead of returning to the thriving city of Philadelphia, Matilda returns to a place that looks dead. There are dead bodies and trenches of graves everywhere, little food to go around, and they city is no longer safe due to thieves who prey on the weak and dead.

7. Why is it difficult for farmers to come to Philadelphia to sell food?
    Farmers have trouble getting into the city since more and more places restrict people from traveling into the city.

8. Why is Matilda so against calling a doctor to help William, Robert, and Nell?
    Matilda knows the doctor will bleed the children. She feels that the French doctors at Bush Hill are more successful in curing yellow fever, and they do not bleed patients. She suspects bleeding patients makes the sickness worse.

Fever 1793 Short Answer Unit Test 1 Answer Key Page 3

9. Why does Matilda need a lawyer to make Eliza a full partner of the coffeehouse?
    Many people in society will think that Eliza, being black, took advantage of the young white girl. Too many people don't like to see black people move up in society, so to be safe they will use a lawyer to it is official.

10. Describe business at the coffeehouse once Matilda takes over.
    Every chair in the coffeehouse is full. They have expanded their menu and hope to soon expand the business. Matilda has proved to be a very successful businesswoman.

III. Vocabulary
   Write in the words you choose for the vocabulary section of the test.

1.

2.

3.

4.

5.

6.

7.

8.

9.

10.

IV. Essay

Grade the essay according to your own criteria.

SHORT ANSWER UNIT TEST 2 - *Fever 1793*

I. Matching/Identify

____ 1. Rev. Allen   A. Woman who gives her services to help others in need

____ 2. Ogilvie   B. Man who changed Bush Hill into a safe place

____ 3. Washington   C. Man whose medical practices harm people more than help

____ 4. Mrs. Flagg   D. Father of two children; lost his wife to the fever

____ 5. Nathaniel   E. Worst way to cure yellow fever

____ 6. Farm   F. Painter Matilda flirts with

____ 7. Mother   G. Place where French doctors work to heal fever victims

____ 8. Dr. Rush   H. Family Matilda's mother hopes her daughter can marry into

____ 9. Bush Hill   I. Capitol of the United States at the time

____ 10. Grandfather   J. Widow who owns a respectable coffeehouse

____ 11. Bleeding   K. People who are making money off fever victims

____ 12. Coffeehouse   L. Best way to stop the spread of the fever

____ 13. Apothecary   M. Person that nurses Matilda back to health from the fever

____ 14. Frost   N. Child who lost her mother to the fever and lives with Matilda

____ 15. Girard   O. Man who organized help for people stuck in Philadelphia

____ 16. Philadelphia   P. Helps Matilda defend her home from robbers

____ 17. Joseph   Q. Social gathering spot to talk news and politics

____ 18. Eliza   R. General Matilda's grandfather served under

____ 19. Nell   S. Refuses to believe that the disease spreading is yellow fever

____ 20. Sword   T. Place where Matilda's mother has been

Fever 1793 Short Answer Unit Test 2 Page 2

II. Short Answer

1. What future does Matilda dream of for herself?

2. Describe the differences in lower, middle, and upper class people in Matilda's city.

3. Matilda's grandfather has finally decided it is time to flee the city to get away from the spread of yellow fever. Why can't Matilda's mother travel with them?

4. What does Matilda's grandfather do while she is recovering at Bush Hill?

5. Matilda is helping out at Eliza's house, acting more like an adult with each passing day. Explain three ways Matilda is acting more mature.

Fever 1793 Short Answer Unit Test 2 Page 3

6. Why is it difficult for farmers to come to Philadelphia to sell food?

7. Why do Eliza and Matilda drag all the furniture outside to the garden?

8. Why is Matilda annoyed at all the people returning from the country?

9. Describe business at the coffeehouse after Matilda takes over.

10. People have been returning to Philadelphia and the town is coming alive once again. What event sparks a massive return to the city for all the remaining people in the country?

Fever 1793 Short Answer Unit Test 2 Page 4

IV. Vocabulary

Write down the vocabulary words. Go back later and write down the correct definition for each word.

	Word	Definition
1		
2		
3		
4		
5		
6		
7		
8		
9		
10		

Fever 1793 Short Answer Unit Test 2 Page 5

IV. Essay: Select *one* of the following topics and respond in an essay.

At the beginning of the novel Matilda is a teenager, and yet at the end she is a successful businesswoman. Trace Matilda's progress in moving from childhood to adulthood over the course of the novel.

OR

"Though we were all healed of the fever, some wounds were inside the heart and would mend slowly." What does Matilda mean by this?

SHORT ANSWER UNIT TEST 2 ANSWER KEY – *Fever 1793*

I. Matching/Identify

O	1. Rev. Allen	A. Woman who gives her services to help others in need
H	2. Ogilvie	B. Man who changed Bush Hill into a safe place
R	3. Washington	C. Man whose medical practices harm people more than help
M	4. Mrs. Flagg	D. Father of two children; lost his wife to the fever
F	5. Nathaniel	E. Worst way to cure yellow fever
T	6. Farm	F. Painter Matilda flirts with
J	7. Mother	G. Place where French doctors work to heal fever victims
C	8. Dr. Rush	H. Family Matilda's mother hopes her daughter can marry into
G	9. Bush Hill	I. Capitol of the United States at the time
S	10. Grandfather	J. Widow who owns a respectable coffeehouse
E	11. Bleeding	K. People who are making money off fever victims
Q	12. Coffeehouse	L. Best way to stop the spread of the fever
K	13. Apothecary	M. Person that nurses Matilda back to health from the fever
L	14. Frost	N. Child who lost her mother to the fever and lives with Matilda
B	15. Girard	O. Man who organized help for people stuck in Philadelphia
I	16. Philadelphia	P. Helps Matilda defend her home from robbers
D	17. Joseph	Q. Social gathering spot to talk news and politics
A	18. Eliza	R. General Matilda's grandfather served under
N	19. Nell	S. Refuses to believe that the disease spreading is yellow fever
P	20. Sword	T. Place where Matilda's mother has been

Fever 1793 Short Answer Unit Test 2 Answer Key Page 2

II. Short Answer

1. What future does Matilda dream of for herself?
    Matilda dreams of traveling to France to bring back beautiful fabric, combs, and jewelry to sell in her own dry goods store. She also dreams of owning a whole block of other businesses including a restaurant, apothecary, school, and hatter's shop.

2. Describe the differences in lower, middle, and upper class people in Matilda's city.
    The lower class people have no where to go to get any type of health care. They are crammed into areas by the wharf and are just waiting to die. Many people blame the illness on them. The middle class people are stuck in the middle. They can get a doctor, but are still uncertain whether to leave their businesses or stay to try and earn more money. The upper class people have fled to their country homes to avoid getting sick.

3. Matilda's grandfather has finally decided it is time to flee the city to get away from the spread of yellow fever. Why can't Matilda's mother travel with them?
    Other towns turn away all fever victims. There is no town that will allow her mother to enter.

4. What does Matilda's grandfather do while she is recovering at Bush Hill?
    Matilda's grandfather keeps busy by organizing the delivery of food to people at Bush Hill, burning filthy mattresses, and helping create ways to raise money to care for the sick.

5. Matilda is helping out at Eliza's house, acting more like an adult with each passing day. Explain three ways Matilda is acting more mature.
    Matilda is giving up her portion of the food so that the younger children can eat, she is doing chores around the house and taking very little time to rest, she travels with Eliza to help sick people until she is weak from exhaustion, and she tries to do the right thing when it comes to taking care of Nell.

6. Why is it difficult for farmers to come to Philadelphia to sell food?
    Farmers have trouble getting into the city since more and more places restrict people from traveling into the city.

7. Why do Eliza and Matilda drag all the furniture outside to the garden?
    There has been a frost overnight and Eliza wants the furniture outside so when another frost comes, the germs on all of the household items will be killed, allowing the house to be rid of yellow fever.

Fever 1793 Short Answer Unit Test 2 Answer Key Page 3

8. Why is Matilda annoyed at all the people returning from the country?
   Matilda feels like they are full of happiness with no thought to the suffering they escaped when they fled.

9. Describe business at the coffeehouse once Matilda takes over.
   Every chair in the coffeehouse is full. They have expanded their menu and hope to soon expand the business. Matilda has proved to be a very successful businesswoman.

10. People have been returning to Philadelphia and the town is coming alive once again. What event sparks a massive return to the city for all the remaining people in the country?
    When President George Washington returns to the city all the remaining people in the country know it must be safe to come back too.

III. Vocabulary
   Write the vocabulary words you have chosen for the test.

1.

2.

3.

4.

5.

6.

7.

8.

9.

10.

IV. Essay: Grade the essay according to your own criteria.

ADVANCED SHORT ANSWER UNIT TEST *Fever 1793*

I. Matching/Identify

____ 1. Rev. Allen   A. Woman who gives her services to help others in need

____ 2. Ogilvie   B. Man who changed Bush Hill into a safe place

____ 3. Washington   C. Man whose medical practices harm people more than help

____ 4. Mrs. Flagg   D. Father of two children; lost his wife to the fever

____ 5. Nathaniel   E. Worst way to cure yellow fever

____ 6. Farm   F. Painter Matilda flirts with

____ 7. Mother   G. Place where French doctors work to heal fever victims

____ 8. Dr. Rush   H. Family Matilda's mother hopes her daughter can marry into

____ 9. Bush Hill   I. Capitol of the United States at the time

____ 10. Grandfather   J. Widow who owns a respectable coffeehouse

____ 11. Bleeding   K. People who are making money off fever victims

____ 12. Coffeehouse   L. Best way to stop the spread of the fever

____ 13. Apothecary   M. Person that nurses Matilda back to health from the fever

____ 14. Frost   N. Child who lost her mother to the fever and lives with Matilda

____ 15. Girard   O. Man who organized help for people stuck in Philadelphia

____ 16. Philadelphia   P. Helps Matilda defend her home from robbers

____ 17. Joseph   Q. Social gathering spot to talk news and politics

____ 18. Eliza   R. General Matilda's grandfather served under

____ 19. Nell   S. Refuses to believe that the disease spreading is yellow fever

____ 20. Sword   T. Place where Matilda's mother has been

Fever 1793 Advanced Short Answer Unit Test Page 2

II. Short Answer

1. Compare and contrast the way Matilda's mother feels about the possibility of a fever spreading with the way her grandfather feels. Who does Matilda side with?

2. Matilda's mother says, "It's not too early to search for a suitable man. With your manners, it could take years." How does Matilda's mother's plan for her future differ from the one Matilda envisions?

3. The elite people in society blame the spread of illness on the lower class. The wealthy are also able to travel away from the city to avoid sickness. What does this say about the class differences in society?

4. Why are the doctors at Bush Hill able to cure yellow fever victims, while other doctors are unable to save anyone from dying?

Fever 1793 Advanced Short Answer Unit Test Page 3

5. "Eliza wouldn't go. She has family here and would have wanted to help. You know Eliza would never run from trouble." Compare and contrast the way Eliza is treated in society because of the color of her skin with the way she treats others in that same society.

6. Throughout the novel Matilda has felt that she was more of a bother and disappointment to her mother than someone her mother could love and be proud of. How does the reader know that Matilda's outlook on how her mother feels about her is not true?

7. At the beginning of the novel Matilda is a teenager, and yet at the end she is a successful businesswoman. Trace Matilda's progress in moving from childhood to adulthood over the course of the novel.

Fever 1793 Advanced Short Answer Unit Test Page 4

III. Vocabulary

Write down the vocabulary words given, then write a paragraph or two about *Speak* correctly using all of the words.

1.	5.	9.
2.	6.	10.
3.	7.	11.
4.	8.	12.

Fever 1793 Advanced Short Answer Unit Test Page 5

IV. Essay

Though the epidemic of yellow fever was tragic, it also helped shape Matilda's life. Discuss the ways in which the tragedy in Philadelphia helped Matilda grow as an individual, then compare and contrast how her life may have gone had she never undergone such a life-altering event.

MULTIPLE CHOICE UNIT TEST 1 - *Fever 1793*

I. Matching/Identify

____ 1. Joseph   A. People who are making money off fever victims

____ 2. Coffeehouse   B. Family Matilda's mother hopes her daughter can marry into

____ 3. Mother   C. General Matilda's grandfather served under

____ 4. Nell   D. Place where Matilda's mother has been

____ 5. Ogilvie   E. Person that nurses Matilda back to health from the fever

____ 6. Bush Hill   F. Painter Matilda flirts with

____ 7. Mrs. Flagg   G. Social gathering spot to talk news and politics

____ 8. Frost   H. Man whose medical practices harm people more than help

____ 9. Nathaniel   I. Man who organized help for people stuck in Philadelphia

____ 10. Eliza   J. Child who lost her mother to the fever and lives with Matilda

____ 11. Apothecary   K. Man who changed Bush Hill into a safe place

____ 12. Farm   L. Helps Matilda defend her home from robbers

____ 13. Bleeding   M. Father of two children; lost his wife to the fever

____ 14. Rev. Allen   N. Capitol of the United States during this time

____ 15. Dr. Rush   O. Woman who gives her services to help others in need

____ 16. Washington   P. Worst way to cure yellow fever

____ 17. Girard   Q. Widow who owns a respectable coffeehouse

____ 18. Grandfather   R. Refuses to believe that the disease spreading is yellow fever

____ 19. Philadelphia   S. Place where French doctors work to heal fever victims

____ 20. Sword   T. Best way to stop the spread of the fever

Fever 1793 Multiple Choice Unit Test 1 Page 2

1. What future does Matilda dream of for herself?
   A. She wants to be married to a rich and noble gentleman.
   B. She want to travel to France and one day own several businesses of her own.
   C. She wants to move to the country where she can enjoy the scenery and fresh air.
   D. She wants to take over the family business and eventually pass it on to her children.

2. Aside from telling the time, why do the church bells ring?
   A. To signify the start of another church service
   B. To signify someone has just given birth
   C. To signify someone has just been married
   D. To signify another person has died

3. Which of the following correctly expresses how BOTH Matilda's mother and grandfather feel about the spread of disease?
   A. Matilda's mother and grandfather both feel safe in the city as long as they stay away from the wharves.
   B. Matilda's mother wants to go to the country, but her grandfather wants to stay in the city.
   C. Matilda's mother wants to stay in the city, but her grandfather wants to go to the country.
   D. Matilda's mother and grandfather both want to go to the country for safety.

4. How do Matilda and her grandfather end up stranded on the side of the road?
   A. The wagon they are traveling in has a broken axle, and no one has the money to make the repair.
   B. The roads are all closed to reduce the spread of fever. The family they are traveling with decides to head back while Matilda and her grandfather decide to find another way.
   C. The men on horseback think Matilda's grandfather has yellow fever, so they refuse to let him in the town. The family dumps them on the road and goes on without them.
   D. Two people in the family they are traveling with get yellow fever. Matilda and her grandfather fear for their lives and decide to wait on the road for another wagon.

5. Why is Matilda terrified to be at Bush Hill?
   A. She has heard it is a dangerous place full of thieves.
   B. She is terrified by how dirty the area is and thinks she might get sick.
   C. She knows if she is there she will probably die.
   D. She sees a man get murdered and fears for her own life.

Fever 1793 Multiple Choice Unit Test 1 Page 3

6. Describe Philadelphia when Matilda and her grandfather return.
   A. There is little food and the city is no longer safe.
   B. Most people have returned from the country, and businesses are open once again.
   C. The city has fire damage since people burned houses of the dead to end the fever.
   D. Almost everyone is homeless since most businesses are now hospitals.

7. Why is it difficult for farmers to come to Philadelphia to sell food?
   A. Farmers have caught the fever too and several are dying, leaving few left to help harvest the food to sell in the city.
   B. Animals are now getting sick with the fever, leaving almost no meat for anyone.
   C. Farmers do not have enough help to take care of their crops, and the drought is killing almost everything, leaving no leftover food to take to the city.
   D. Farmers are not allowed to travel in and out of the city due to restrictions placed by the government to avoid the spread of the fever.

8. Why is Matilda so against calling a doctor to help William, Robert, and Nell?
   A. She knows that Eliza and her family will not have the money to pay. She doesn't want them to sacrifice their home in order to get help.
   B. She knows he will bleed the children. After seeing how the French doctors at Bush Hill treated patients, she realizes that bleeding only makes the fever worse.
   C. She knows that several doctors are really uneducated. Several are drunks who can do nothing to help.
   D. She knows that the doctors will try to take advantage of a young girl and a black woman, so she fears they may regret the decision later.

9. Why does Matilda need a lawyer to make Eliza a full partner of the coffeehouse?
   A. Matilda is drawing up a complicated plan that will make Eliza a partner. However, the first several years of her profits will go straight to Matilda until she has paid for her half of the coffeehouse. Since this may be confusing, a lawyer is needed to keep it straight.
   B. There is worry about what will happen if Matilda's mother comes back or Matilda changes her mind. In order to make sure Eliza gets what she deserves, a lawyer is needed to make permanent changes.
   C. With the establishment of the new American government, there is now a law requiring all business owners to register and pay taxes. A lawyer is needed to make sure the proper paperwork is filled out.
   D. Too many people will think that Eliza, being black, took advantage of the young, white girl. White people don't usually like to see black people move up in society and to avoid any trouble a lawyer is needed to make it official.

Fever 1793 Multiple Choice Unit Test 1 Page 4

10. Describe business at the coffeehouse after Matilda takes over.
    A. Every chair in the coffeehouse is full. They have expanded the menu and Matilda has proven to be a very successful businesswoman.
    B. Business is starting to pick up. The coffeehouse is not full, but Eliza and Matilda are able to support themselves.
    C. Business is slow since many people have not yet returned from the country.
    D. The business has gone bankrupt and Matilda will have to marry in order to survive.

Fever 1793 Multiple Choice Unit Test 1 Page 5

III. Essay
Select *one* of the following topics and respond in an essay:

Eliza tells Matilda, "You can only climb one mountain at a time." What does she mean by this? How does Matilda "climb one mountain at a time" throughout the story?

OR

Even though it seems like a charitable thing to do, Matilda admits that taking care of Nell is selfish. How is this true?

Fever 1793 Multiple Choice Unit Test 1 Page 6

IV. Vocabulary - Match the correct definitions to the words.

____ 1. Wharves   A. A sickly person; someone who is too weak to care for himself

____ 2. Loitering   B. The yellow discoloration of the skin due to disease

____ 3. Exorbitant   C. To envy or resent the good fortune of someone else

____ 4. Implore   D. Swiftness of motion; hurry; rush; go with speed

____ 5. Fetid   E. Marked with great energy or passion

____ 6. Impudence   F. Extremely thin and boney

____ 7. Taut   G. A deadly disease

____ 8. Destitute   H. Food fit for humans to eat

____ 9. Begrudge   I. To linger aimlessly; to hang about; to delay

____ 10. Vehemently   J. Having an offensive odor

____ 11. Haste   K. The quality of being offensively bold; nerve; rudeness

____ 12. Invalid   L. Tightly drawn or tense

____ 13. Proprietor   M. A landing place where ships may tie up and load or unload

____ 14. Salvage   N. Cleanse; purify; get rid of something impure

____ 15. Pestilence   O. Excessive; extreme; unreasonable

____ 16. Jaundiced   P. Alone or unattended

____ 17. Purge   Q. Lacking food, clothing, and shelter; poor; impoverished

____ 18. Gaunt   R. To beg urgently

____ 19. Victuals   S. The act of saving or rescuing

____ 20. Solitary   T. Owner of a business establishment

MULTIPLE CHOICE UNIT TEST 2 – *Fever 1793*

I. Matching/Identify

_____ 1. Rev. Allen   A. Woman who gives her services to help others in need

_____ 2. Ogilvie   B. Man who changed Bush Hill into a safe place

_____ 3. Washington   C. Man whose medical practices harm people more than help

_____ 4. Mrs. Flagg   D. Father of two children; lost his wife to the fever

_____ 5. Nathaniel   E. Worst way to cure yellow fever

_____ 6. Farm   F. Painter Matilda flirts with

_____ 7. Mother   G. Place where French doctors work to heal fever victims

_____ 8. Dr. Rush   H. Family Matilda's mother hopes her daughter can marry into

_____ 9. Bush Hill   I. Capitol of the United States at the time

_____ 10. Grandfather   J. Widow who owns a respectable coffeehouse

_____ 11. Bleeding   K. People who are making money off fever victims

_____ 12. Coffeehouse   L. Best way to stop the spread of the fever

_____ 13. Apothecary   M. Person that nurses Matilda back to health from the fever

_____ 14. Frost   N. Child who lost her mother to the fever and lives with Matilda

_____ 15. Girard   O. Man who organized help for people stuck in Philadelphia

_____ 16. Philadelphia   P. Helps Matilda defend her home from robbers

_____ 17. Joseph   Q. Social gathering spot to talk news and politics

_____ 18. Eliza   R. General Matilda's grandfather served under

_____ 19. Nell   S. Refuses to believe that the disease spreading is yellow fever

_____ 20. Sword   T. Place where Matilda's mother has been

Fever 1793 Multiple Choice Unit Test 2 Page 2

1. What future does Matilda dream of for herself?
    A. She wants to be married to a rich and noble gentleman.
    B. She want to travel to France and one day own several businesses of her own.
    C. She wants to move to the country where she can enjoy the scenery and fresh air.
    D. She wants to take over the family business and eventually pass it on to her children.

2. Which of the following correctly describes the differences between the lower, middle, and upper class people in Matilda's city?
    A. The lower class have no where to get health care, the middle class can't decide whether to leave their businesses or stay to make money, and the upper class flee to the country for safety.
    B. The lower class are all dying quickly, the middle class are able to get health care and survive without any problems, and the upper class are fleeing to the country.
    C. The lower class are fleeing to the country, the middle class can't decide whether to leave their businesses or stay to make money, and the upper class can afford good health care while remaining in the city.
    D. The lower class are all dying quickly, the middle class are fleeing to the country, and the upper class can afford good heath care while remaining in the city.

3. Matilda's grandfather has finally decided it is time to flee the city to get away from the spread of yellow fever. Why can't Matilda's mother travel with them?
    A. She is too confused to understand and refuses to go.
    B. Travel is expensive and there isn't enough money for all three people to go.
    C. Other towns won't allow people with yellow fever to enter.
    D. She is too sick to travel; it would surely kill her.

4. What does Matilda's grandfather do while she is recovering?
    A. Delivers food, burns dirty mattresses, and helps figure out how to raise more money
    B. Carries dead bodies to the fire where they are cremated
    C. Helps children who lost their parents to yellow fever find a new home
    D. Hangs out in the barn trying to recover from his own illness

5. Matilda is helping out at Eliza's house, acting more like an adult with each passing day. In what ways Matilda is acting more mature?
    A. She legally adopted Nell, is working to restore the coffeehouse, and is considering getting married.
    B. She gives up her portion of food to feed the children, asks for extra chores, and is helping care for fever victims.
    C. She is cooking all the meals, caring for all three children by herself, and working to restore the coffeehouse.
    D. She is learning to sew and mend clothing, considering marriage, and taking a leadership role in Reverend Allen's organization.

Fever 1793 Multiple Choice Unit Test 2 Page 3

6. Why is it difficult for farmers to come to Philadelphia to sell food?
    A. Farmers have caught the fever, too, and several are dying, leaving few left to help harvest the food to sell in the city.
    B. Animals are now getting sick with the fever, leaving almost no meat for anyone.
    C. Farmers do not have enough help to take care of their crops, and the drought is killing almost everything, leaving no leftover food to take to the city.
    D. Farmers are not allowed to travel in and out of the city due to restrictions placed by the government to avoid the spread of the fever.

7. Why do Eliza and Matilda drag all the furniture outside to the garden?
    A. They are forced to stay out the garden since the house is too hot.
    B. They want the coffeehouse to look empty from the street so no one else will rob it.
    C. They want to kill all the yellow fever germs by placing it outside for the next frost.
    D. They need to wash it all off, and that will be easier to do in the garden next to the well.

8. Why is Matilda annoyed at all the people returning from the country?
    A. She feels like they are happy, well-fed, and giving no thought to the suffering anyone else endured.
    B. She feels like they are bragging about how rich they are and how much fun it was to take a vacation from the city; she is a little jealous.
    C. She hears them saying bad things about black people and gets defensive since she has been living in the black community for the last couple of months.
    D. She liked the city when it wasn't as crowded and noisy.

9. People have been returning to Philadelphia and the town is coming alive once again. What event sparks a massive return to the city for all the remaining people in the country?
    A. When the market reopens, that is a sign that the fever is over and people are safe to return to the city.
    B. When President George Washington returns to the city, all the remaining people in the country know it must be safe to return, too.
    C. When there is a town meeting called, everyone knows it is safe to return form the country.
    D. When the first heavy snowfall comes at Christmas, people know the fever is gone.

10. Describe business at the coffeehouse after Matilda takes over.
    A. Every chair in the coffeehouse is full. They have expanded the menu and Matilda has proven to be a very successful businesswoman.
    B. Business is starting to pick up. The coffeehouse is not full, but Eliza and Matilda are able to support themselves.
    C. Business is slow since many people have not yet returned from the country.
    D. The business has gone bankrupt and Matilda will have to marry in order to survive.

Fever 1793 Multiple Choice Unit Test 2 Page 4

III. Vocabulary - Match the correct definitions to the words.

_____ 1. Impudence   A. A sickly person; someone who is too weak to care for himself

_____ 2. Instill   B. The yellow discoloration of the skin due to disease

_____ 3. Vehemently   C. To envy or resent the good fortune of someone else

_____ 4. Placid   D. A noisy commotion or disturbance

_____ 5. Invalid   E. Marked with great energy or passion

_____ 6. Vanity   F. Serious; sober; gloomy

_____ 7. Begrudge   G. A deadly disease

_____ 8. Abide   H. Food fit for humans to eat

_____ 9. Bestir   I. To gradually put something into someone's mind or feelings

_____ 10. Putrid   J. Having an offensive odor

_____ 11. Wharves   K. The quality of being offensively bold; nerve; rudeness

_____ 12. Ruckus   L. To accept to put up with; to tolerate

_____ 13. Solemn   M. A landing place where ships may tie up and load or unload

_____ 14. Fetid   N. In a state of foul decay; rotten

_____ 15. Pestilence   O. Excessive; extreme; unreasonable

_____ 16. Jaundiced   P. Excessive pride in one's appearance

_____ 17. Exorbitant   Q. Lacking food, clothing, and shelter; poor; impoverished

_____ 18. Proprietor   R. Quiet; calm; peaceful

_____ 19. Victuals   S. To stir up, rouse, or bring to action

_____ 20. Destitute   T. Owner of a business establishment

Fever 1793 Multiple Choice Unit Test 2 Page 5

IV. Essay: Select *one* of the following topics and respond in an essay.

List five of Matilda's most important character traits and give examples of each.

OR

Tell what you think Laurie Halse Anderson wanted you to learn from reading this book. Use specific examples from the book to support your answer.

ANSWER SHEET - *Fever 1793*

	Matching	Mult. Choice	Vocabulary
1			
2			
3			
4			
5			
6			
7			
8			
9			
10			
11			
12			
13			
14			
15			
16			
17			
18			
19			
20			

MULTIPLE CHOICE UNIT TEST 1 ANSWER KEY - *Fever 1793*

	Matching	Mult. Choice	Vocabulary
1	M	B	M
2	G	D	I
3	Q	B	O
4	J	C	R
5	B	A	J
6	S	A	K
7	E	D	L
8	T	B	Q
9	F	D	C
10	O	A	E
11	A		D
12	D		A
13	P		T
14	I		S
15	H		G
16	C		B
17	K		N
18	R		F
19	N		H
20	L		P

MULTIPLE CHOICE UNIT TEST 2 ANSWER KEY - *Fever 1793*

	Matching	Mult. Choice	Vocabulary
1	O	B	K
2	H	A	I
3	R	C	E
4	M	A	R
5	F	B	A
6	T	D	P
7	J	C	C
8	C	A	L
9	G	B	S
10	S	A	N
11	E		M
12	Q		D
13	K		F
14	L		J
15	B		G
16	I		B
17	D		O
18	A		T
19	N		H
20	P		Q

UNIT RESOURCE MATERIALS

BULLETIN BOARD IDEAS - *Fever 1793*

1. Save one corner of the board for the best of students' *Fever 1793* writing assignments.

2. Take one of the word search puzzles from the extra activities packet and with a marker copy it over in a large size on the bulletin board. Write the clue words to find to one side. Invite students prior to and after class to find the words and circle them on the bulletin board.

3. Write several of the most significant quotations from the book onto the board on brightly colored paper.

4. Make a bulletin board listing the vocabulary words for this unit. As you complete sections of the novel and discuss the vocabulary for each section, write the definitions on the bulletin board. (If your board is one students face frequently, it will help them learn the words.)

5. Decorate your bulletin board with information about the time period. Put examples of clothing, trades, transportation, etc on the bulletin board to help students learn about the late 1700s.

6. Turn your bulletin board into a map of Philadelphia. Put the streets Matilda talks about on the map and mark locations like the market, the coffeehouse, the wharves, etc.

7. Put pictures of the prominent historical figures Laurie Halse Anderson quotes at the start of each chapter. Post additional information about these people for students to have a better understanding of who these men were.

8. Make a bulletin board advertising other young adult historical fiction novels. Print out colorful copies of the covers of these other historical fiction novels and attach a short summary or excerpt.

9. Make a bulletin board with colorful copies of Laurie Halse Anderson's other novels. Write a short tease for the book to get students interested.

10. Post information regarding yellow fever today. Several maps are available online showing areas where yellow fever deaths still occur. You may also want to post information regarding the disease on your bulletin board as well.

EXTRA ACTIVITIES - *Fever 1793*

One of the difficulties in teaching a novel is that all students don't read at the same speed. One student who likes to read may take the book home and finish it in a day or two. Sometimes a few students finish the in-class assignments early. The problem, then, is finding suitable extra activities for students.

One thing that seems to help is to keep a little library in the classroom. For this unit on *Fever 1793*, you might check out from the school library *Catalyst, Prom, Twisted,* or *Speak,* other novels by Laurie Halse Anderson. Other historical fiction novels for teens would be good titles to have in your room as well. Articles or books about the city of Philadelphia (travel guides, maps, newspapers), yellow fever and other contagious diseases, disasters or plagues (recent or past), careers (in medicine, the restaurant business, world-aid organizations), volunteer groups and opportunities, or civil rights would be good additions to an in-class library.

Other things you may keep on hand are puzzles. We have made some relating directly to *Fever 1793* for you. Feel free to duplicate them for your students to use.

Some students may like to draw. You might devise a contest or allow some extra-credit grade for students who draw characters or scenes from *Fever 1793*. Note, too, that if the students do not want to keep their drawings you may pick up some extra bulletin board materials this way. If you have a contest and you supply the prize (a free iTune download or something like that perhaps), you could, possibly, make the drawing itself a non-returnable entry fee.

The pages which follow contain games, puzzles and worksheets. The keys, when appropriate, immediately follow the puzzle or worksheet. There are two main groups of activities: one group for the unit; that is, generally relating to *Fever 1793* text, and another group of activities related strictly to *Fever 1793* vocabulary.

Directions for these games, puzzles and worksheets are self-explanatory. The object here is to provide you with extra materials you may use in any way you choose.

MORE ACTIVITIES - *Fever 1793*

1. Have students work together to make a time line chronology of the events in the story. Take a large piece of construction paper and on one wall (or however you can physically arrange it in your room) make the events of the story along it. Students may want to add drawings or cut-out pictures to represent the events (as well as a written statement).

2. Have students design a book cover (front and back and inside flaps) for *Fever 1793*.

3. Have students design a bulletin board (ready to be put up; not just sketched) for *Fever 1793*.

4. Have students choose one chapter of the book (with sufficient dialogue) to rewrite as a play. In conjunction with this assignment, have students write a composition explaining the difficulties they encountered in changing from one written form to another.

5. Have students write out the characters in the book and cast famous actors and actress for a movie version of the novel. Instruct students to write a brief explanation as to why the actor/actress they selected would be perfect for the part.

6. Matilda constantly mentions streets names along with the places she frequents in her city. Have students make a map of their own city and mark places that are memorable or important to them.

7. There are several foods mentioned in the novel that students are unfamiliar with. Have students research foods of that time period. Provide the class with a day students can bring in samples of the food from the time period to share.

8. Allow students to explore Laurie Halse Anderson's web page (www.writerlady.com).

9. Have students write a short sequel, discussing what happens to Matilda and her family business once her mother returns.

10. Have students find a poem that has the same topic/theme as *Fever 1793*. Tell students to put the text of the poem on a paper and make a collage of magazine word/picture cutouts to decorate the area around the poem.

11. Have students create ways to expand their humanitarian project from the school to the community. Have them make a plan to get local businesses involved in raising money/supplies and put it into action.

12. Have students select a character from the book and complete the "I Am" poem from that character's point of view. (see handout on following page)

"I Am" Poem

Complete this "I am" poem. You may select any character from the book to do this poem about. Be sure to write from his or her point of view and think about the things he or she would feel. You may use some short one word answers, but do not make each line only a few words. You should try to provide support from the novel to really develop this poem so that it reveals information and insight about the character you select.

I am (2 characteristics your character has)
I wonder (something your character wonders)
I hear (something real or imaginary your character hears)
I see (something real or imaginary your character sees)
I want (something your character desires)
I am (the first line of the poem repeated)

I pretend (something your character pretends to do)
I feel (something real or imaginary your character feels emotionally)
I touch (something real or imaginary your character would touch physically)
I worry (something your characters worries about)
I cry (something that makes your character upset)
I am (the first line of the poem repeated)

I understand (something your character knows)
I say (something your character believes in)
I dream (something your character would dream about)
I try (something your character makes an effort to do)
I hope (something your character hopes for)
I am (the first line of the poem repeated)

WORD LIST - Fever 1793

No.	Word	Clue/Definition
1.	ANDERSON	Author
2.	BATHE	Matilda does this once a month and on special occasions.
3.	BELLS	These ring whenever someone dies.
4.	BIBLE	Matilda likes to read it at the end of each day.
5.	BUSH	Matilda is taken to ___ Hill to recover from yellow fever.
6.	CART	A man dumps Matilda's mother off of one.
7.	CHURN	Chore to keep the children busy: ___ butter
8.	COLETTE	Eloped with her French tutor
9.	COUNTRY	Wealthy people flee there to escape the fever.
10.	DOWRY	Joseph thinks Matilda should sell the coffeehouse so she has a nice ___.
11.	ELIZA	Coffeehouse partner with Matilda
12.	FATHER	He fell off a ladder and died of a broken neck.
13.	FLAGG	Grandfather flirts with her as she nurses Matilda back to health.
14.	FLOWERS	Nathaniel Benson throws these out a window at Matilda and Eliza.
15.	FRANCE	Country Matilda wants to go to
16.	FRENCH	These doctors know how to treat the fever better than anyone else.
17.	FROST	It kills off the mosquitoes and the yellow fever.
18.	GARDEN	Place Matilda's grandfather wants her to get their food
19.	GEORGE	Parrot's name: King ___
20.	GIRARD	Stephen ___ turns Bush Hill into a safe hospital.
21.	JEFFERSON	Matilda wants to get Thomas ___ to eat at the coffeehouse.
22.	JOSEPH	Eliza's brother who lost his wife to yellow fever
23.	LUDINGTON	Family whose farm Matilda's mother wants to send her to
24.	MARKET	Place where people buy and sell food
25.	MOTHER	She is assumed dead but comes back to the coffeehouse at the end.
26.	NELL	Small child Matilda finds and cares for
27.	OGILVIE	Family Matilda's mother hopes her daughter can marry into
28.	ORPHANAGE	Place the people at Bush Hill want Matilda to go to help out
29.	PAINTER	Nathaniel Benson's job
30.	PEALE	Nathaniel sends Matilda a note saying he is safe at ___'s house.
31.	PEARS	Matilda is gathering these when she passes out, sick with the fever
32.	POLLY	Girl who worked at the coffeehouse who dies of yellow fever
33.	PORTRAIT	Item Matilda buries with her grandfather
34.	PRAYER	Matilda has to fight to get one said at her grandfather's funeral.
35.	REFUGEES	People Matilda's grandfather thinks are to blame for the fever
36.	ROBBED	Matilda and her grandfather return to Philadelphia & discover they were ___.
37.	RUSH	He believes black people can't catch yellow fever.
38.	SAWDUST	People mixed it with flour to make more bread.
39.	SILAS	The cat's name
40.	SKIRT	Matilda uses this to try to catch fish.
41.	STRONGBOX	Hiding place for coffeehouse money
42.	SWORD	Matilda stabs the robber with it.
43.	WAGON	Transportation to the country
44.	WALK	What Matilda and Nathaniel do every evening
45.	WASHINGTON	Business grows when George ___ builds a home a few blocks away.
46.	WHARVES	Matilda's mother forbids her to go there for fear she might get sick.
47.	WILLOW	Matilda searches for this kind of a tree, knowing water will be nearby.

WORD SEARCH - Fever 1793

```
B A N D E R S O N W H A R V E S L D K R
A K J M Z M T G P F G G F K P C G X Z E
T S J E L D Z L Y R S R J D O B Y C M F
H D Y F F S T R O N G B O X R D I M D U
E X P F N F T F L U D I N G T O N B P G
Q M Q J L N E R W O K J B Z R H C L L E
N S K S U R Z R R H L W N H A F F T N E
L R J O E F J P S W D A C K I C W R G S
L E C H B D H Z F O F G M O T O U R T T
E W T Y F A G G S R N O Q X L H O T F P
N O T G N I H S A W O N F L C E L A E P
M L N A R G A N W R Z S I L G A T X V N
D F G A G L C Y D M D W T D A H R T R Z
O E R O I E R Z U R G E C K E G L T E M
W D F S G E B U S H O H N R N P G M Y M
R A E R T I M P T S P B P Z E O S A A M
Y S L N E L L D X E W Y B A R L W R R V
T R I K S N Z V S H S U R E K L O K P N
M A Z R X S C O I K C S N P D Y R E G Z
P P A C R H J H Z E P B E L L S D T T P
```

ANDERSON	ELIZA	JEFFERSON	PEARS	STRONGBOX
BATHE	FATHER	JOSEPH	POLLY	SWORD
BELLS	FLAGG	LUDINGTON	PORTRAIT	WAGON
BIBLE	FLOWERS	MARKET	PRAYER	WALK
BUSH	FRANCE	MOTHER	REFUGEES	WASHINGTON
CART	FRENCH	NELL	ROBBED	WHARVES
CHURN	FROST	OGILVIE	RUSH	WILLOW
COLETTE	GARDEN	ORPHANAGE	SAWDUST	
COUNTRY	GEORGE	PAINTER	SILAS	
DOWRY	GIRARD	PEALE	SKIRT	

WORD SEARCH ANSWER KEY - Fever 1793

```
B A N D E R S O N W H A R V E S             R
A       J                           P       E
T       E               Y           O   B   F
H           F   S T R O N G B O X   R   I   U
E           F   T       L U D I N G T O N B G
            N E         O           R       E
        S   U   R   R       W       A       E
    L   R   O   E   P S A   C   I   W R G   S
    L   E   C H     H   F O G   O T O U R
    E   W T     A G G S R N O       L H O   F
    N O T G N I H S A W O N F L C E L A E P
    M   L   A   R   A N W   R S I L G A T
    D F G   A   L C D   D W   T     A R T R
    O E R O I E R   U   R   E   E   G T E
    W D F S G E B U S H O H N R     P G M Y
    R A E R T I     T   P B     E O S A
    Y   L N E     L     E     B A   L W R R
    T R I K S N   V S H S U R E     L O K P
        A Z         C O I     S   D Y R E
    P   A         J H   E   B E L L S D T
```

ANDERSON	ELIZA	JEFFERSON	PEARS	STRONGBOX
BATHE	FATHER	JOSEPH	POLLY	SWORD
BELLS	FLAGG	LUDINGTON	PORTRAIT	WAGON
BIBLE	FLOWERS	MARKET	PRAYER	WALK
BUSH	FRANCE	MOTHER	REFUGEES	WASHINGTON
CART	FRENCH	NELL	ROBBED	WHARVES
CHURN	FROST	OGILVIE	RUSH	WILLOW
COLETTE	GARDEN	ORPHANAGE	SAWDUST	
COUNTRY	GEORGE	PAINTER	SILAS	
DOWRY	GIRARD	PEALE	SKIRT	

CROSSWORD - Fever 1793

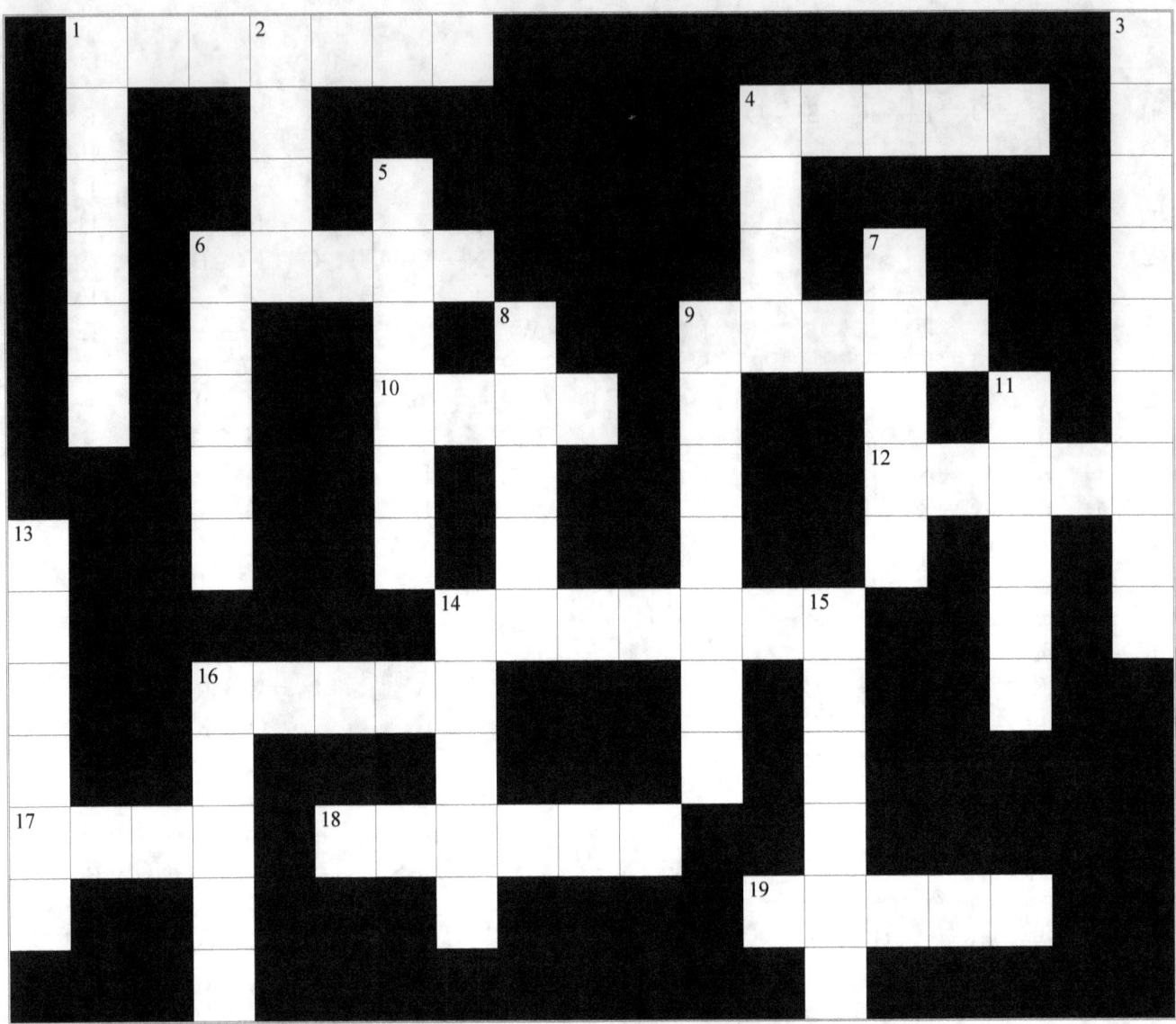

Across
1. Nathaniel Benson throws these out a window at Matilda and Eliza.
4. These ring whenever someone dies.
6. Matilda uses this to try to catch fish.
9. Chore to keep the children busy: ___ butter
10. Small child Matilda finds and cares for
12. The cat's name
14. Nathaniel Benson's job
16. Matilda likes to read it at the end of each day.
17. A man dumps Matilda's mother off of one.
18. Matilda searches for this kind of a tree, knowing water will be nearby.
19. Matilda is gathering these when she passes out, sick with the fever

Down
1. He fell off a ladder and died of a broken neck.
2. What Matilda and Nathaniel do every evening
3. Matilda wants to get Thomas ___ to eat at the coffeehouse.
4. Matilda is taken to ___ Hill to recover from yellow fever.
5. Country Matilda wants to go to
6. Matilda stabs the robber with it.
7. It kills off the mosquitoes and the yellow fever.
8. Coffeehouse partner with Matilda
9. Wealthy people flee there to escape the fever.
11. Grandfather flirts with her as she nurses Matilda back to health.
13. These doctors know how to treat the fever better than anyone else.
14. Nathaniel sends Matilda a note saying he is safe at ___'s house.
15. Matilda and her grandfather return to Philadelphia & discover they were ___.
16. Matilda does this once a month and on special occasions.

CROSSWORD ANSWER KEY - Fever 1793

Across
1. Nathaniel Benson throws these out a window at Matilda and Eliza.
4. These ring whenever someone dies.
6. Matilda uses this to try to catch fish.
9. Chore to keep the children busy: ___ butter
10. Small child Matilda finds and cares for
12. The cat's name
14. Nathaniel Benson's job
16. Matilda likes to read it at the end of each day.
17. A man dumps Matilda's mother off of one.
18. Matilda searches for this kind of a tree, knowing water will be nearby.
19. Matilda is gathering these when she passes out, sick with the fever

Down
1. He fell off a ladder and died of a broken neck.
2. What Matilda and Nathaniel do every evening
3. Matilda wants to get Thomas ___ to eat at the coffeehouse.
4. Matilda is taken to ___ Hill to recover from yellow fever.
5. Country Matilda wants to go to
6. Matilda stabs the robber with it.
7. It kills off the mosquitoes and the yellow fever.
8. Coffeehouse partner with Matilda
9. Wealthy people flee there to escape the fever.
11. Grandfather flirts with her as she nurses Matilda back to health.
13. These doctors know how to treat the fever better than anyone else.
14. Nathaniel sends Matilda a note saying he is safe at ___'s house.
15. Matilda and her grandfather return to Philadelphia & discover they were ___.
16. Matilda does this once a month and on special occasions.

MATCHING 1 - Fever 1793

___ 1. WILLOW   A. Chore to keep the children busy: ___ butter

___ 2. FATHER   B. Wealthy people flee there to escape the fever.

___ 3. FLAGG   C. Transportation to the country

___ 4. PORTRAIT   D. Place the people at Bush Hill want Matilda to go to help out

___ 5. REFUGEES   E. Nathaniel sends Matilda a note saying he is safe at ___'s house.

___ 6. BUSH   F. People mixed it with flour to make more bread.

___ 7. PEALE   G. Hiding place for coffeehouse money

___ 8. FRENCH   H. Eliza's brother who lost his wife to yellow fever

___ 9. ROBBED   I. A man dumps Matilda's mother off of one.

___ 10. SKIRT   J. He fell off a ladder and died of a broken neck.

___ 11. SWORD   K. Matilda is taken to ___ Hill to recover from yellow fever.

___ 12. FLOWERS   L. Matilda stabs the robber with it.

___ 13. ORPHANAGE   M. It kills off the mosquitoes and the yellow fever.

___ 14. MARKET   N. Matilda searches for this kind of a tree, knowing water will be nearby.

___ 15. COUNTRY   O. Place where people buy and sell food

___ 16. JEFFERSON   P. Family Matilda's mother hopes her daughter can marry into

___ 17. FROST   Q. Matilda and her grandfather return to Philadelphia & discover they were ___.

___ 18. JOSEPH   R. Matilda wants to get Thomas ___ to eat at the coffeehouse.

___ 19. CHURN   S. Nathaniel Benson throws these out a window at Matilda and Eliza.

___ 20. CART   T. These doctors know how to treat the fever better than anyone else.

___ 21. SAWDUST   U. Grandfather flirts with her as she nurses Matilda back to health.

___ 22. WAGON   V. People Matilda's grandfather thinks are to blame for the fever

___ 23. STRONGBOX   W. Item Matilda buries with her grandfather

___ 24. OGILVIE   X. Matilda uses this to try to catch fish.

___ 25. BATHE   Y. Matilda does this once a month and on special occasions.

MATCHING 1 ANSWER KEY - Fever 1793

N - 1.	WILLOW	A. Chore to keep the children busy: ___ butter
J - 2.	FATHER	B. Wealthy people flee there to escape the fever.
U - 3.	FLAGG	C. Transportation to the country
W - 4.	PORTRAIT	D. Place the people at Bush Hill want Matilda to go to help out
V - 5.	REFUGEES	E. Nathaniel sends Matilda a note saying he is safe at ___'s house.
K - 6.	BUSH	F. People mixed it with flour to make more bread.
E - 7.	PEALE	G. Hiding place for coffeehouse money
T - 8.	FRENCH	H. Eliza's brother who lost his wife to yellow fever
Q - 9.	ROBBED	I. A man dumps Matilda's mother off of one.
X - 10.	SKIRT	J. He fell off a ladder and died of a broken neck.
L - 11.	SWORD	K. Matilda is taken to ___ Hill to recover from yellow fever.
S - 12.	FLOWERS	L. Matilda stabs the robber with it.
D - 13.	ORPHANAGE	M. It kills off the mosquitoes and the yellow fever.
O - 14.	MARKET	N. Matilda searches for this kind of a tree, knowing water will be nearby.
B - 15.	COUNTRY	O. Place where people buy and sell food
R - 16.	JEFFERSON	P. Family Matilda's mother hopes her daughter can marry into
M - 17.	FROST	Q. Matilda and her grandfather return to Philadelphia & discover they were ___.
H - 18.	JOSEPH	R. Matilda wants to get Thomas ___ to eat at the coffeehouse.
A - 19.	CHURN	S. Nathaniel Benson throws these out a window at Matilda and Eliza.
I - 20.	CART	T. These doctors know how to treat the fever better than anyone else.
F - 21.	SAWDUST	U. Grandfather flirts with her as she nurses Matilda back to health.
C - 22.	WAGON	V. People Matilda's grandfather thinks are to blame for the fever
G - 23.	STRONGBOX	W. Item Matilda buries with her grandfather
P - 24.	OGILVIE	X. Matilda uses this to try to catch fish.
Y - 25.	BATHE	Y. Matilda does this once a month and on special occasions.

MATCHING 2 - Fever 1793

___ 1. ROBBED   A. Business grows when George ___ builds a home a few blocks away.
___ 2. GIRARD   B. Nathaniel Benson's job
___ 3. PEARS   C. The cat's name
___ 4. FROST   D. Grandfather flirts with her as she nurses Matilda back to health.
___ 5. JEFFERSON   E. Matilda wants to get Thomas ___ to eat at the coffeehouse.
___ 6. OGILVIE   F. Matilda's mother forbids her to go there for fear she might get sick.
___ 7. MARKET   G. Matilda searches for this kind of a tree, knowing water will be nearby.
___ 8. SKIRT   H. Nathaniel sends Matilda a note saying he is safe at ___'s house.
___ 9. FATHER   I. Place where people buy and sell food
___ 10. WHARVES   J. Family Matilda's mother hopes her daughter can marry into
___ 11. WILLOW   K. Matilda and her grandfather return to Philadelphia & discover they were ___.
___ 12. SAWDUST   L. Stephen ___ turns Bush Hill into a safe hospital.
___ 13. PEALE   M. A man dumps Matilda's mother off of one.
___ 14. WALK   N. What Matilda and Nathaniel do every evening
___ 15. WAGON   O. He fell off a ladder and died of a broken neck.
___ 16. FLAGG   P. Matilda does this once a month and on special occasions.
___ 17. POLLY   Q. Chore to keep the children busy: ___ butter
___ 18. BATHE   R. It kills off the mosquitoes and the yellow fever.
___ 19. SILAS   S. Transportation to the country
___ 20. WASHINGTON   T. Girl who worked at the coffeehouse who dies of yellow fever
___ 21. LUDINGTON   U. Matilda is taken to ___ Hill to recover from yellow fever.
___ 22. CHURN   V. Matilda uses this to try to catch fish.
___ 23. CART   W. People mixed it with flour to make more bread.
___ 24. PAINTER   X. Family whose farm Matilda's mother wants to send her to
___ 25. BUSH   Y. Matilda is gathering these when she passes out, sick with the fever

MATCHING 2 ANSWER KEY - Fever 1793

K - 1. ROBBED		A. Business grows when George ___ builds a home a few blocks away.
L - 2. GIRARD		B. Nathaniel Benson's job
Y - 3. PEARS		C. The cat's name
R - 4. FROST		D. Grandfather flirts with her as she nurses Matilda back to health.
E - 5. JEFFERSON		E. Matilda wants to get Thomas ___ to eat at the coffeehouse.
J - 6. OGILVIE		F. Matilda's mother forbids her to go there for fear she might get sick.
I - 7. MARKET		G. Matilda searches for this kind of a tree, knowing water will be nearby.
V - 8. SKIRT		H. Nathaniel sends Matilda a note saying he is safe at ___'s house.
O - 9. FATHER		I. Place where people buy and sell food
F -10. WHARVES		J. Family Matilda's mother hopes her daughter can marry into
G -11. WILLOW		K. Matilda and her grandfather return to Philadelphia & discover they were ___.
W 12. SAWDUST		L. Stephen ___ turns Bush Hill into a safe hospital.
H -13. PEALE		M. A man dumps Matilda's mother off of one.
N -14. WALK		N. What Matilda and Nathaniel do every evening
S -15. WAGON		O. He fell off a ladder and died of a broken neck.
D -16. FLAGG		P. Matilda does this once a month and on special occasions.
T -17. POLLY		Q. Chore to keep the children busy: ___ butter
P -18. BATHE		R. It kills off the mosquitoes and the yellow fever.
C -19. SILAS		S. Transportation to the country
A -20. WASHINGTON		T. Girl who worked at the coffeehouse who dies of yellow fever
X -21. LUDINGTON		U. Matilda is taken to ___ Hill to recover from yellow fever.
Q -22. CHURN		V. Matilda uses this to try to catch fish.
M 23. CART		W. People mixed it with flour to make more bread.
B -24. PAINTER		X. Family whose farm Matilda's mother wants to send her to
U -25. BUSH		Y. Matilda is gathering these when she passes out, sick with the fever

JUGGLE LETTERS - Fever 1793

1. LSISA = 1. _____
   The cat's name

2. PSHEJO = 2. _____
   Eliza's brother who lost his wife to yellow fever

3. IGLOTUDNN = 3. _____
   Family whose farm Matilda's mother wants to send her to

4. TRAEMK = 4. _____
   Place where people buy and sell food

5. HASWVRE = 5. _____
   Matilda's mother forbids her to go there for fear she might get sick.

6. ILAZE = 6. _____
   Coffeehouse partner with Matilda

7. GAOEPANRH = 7. _____
   Place the people at Bush Hill want Matilda to go to help out

8. DNEGAR = 8. _____
   Place Matilda's grandfather wants her to get their food

9. ADRIGR = 9. _____
   Stephen ___ turns Bush Hill into a safe hospital.

10. RCTA = 10. _____
    A man dumps Matilda's mother off of one.

11. EFRJEFNSO = 11. _____
    Matilda wants to get Thomas ___ to eat at the coffeehouse.

12. SRHU = 12. _____
    He believes black people can't catch yellow fever.

13. EUSGFEER = 13. _____
    People Matilda's grandfather thinks are to blame for the fever

14. LAEEP = 14. _____
    Nathaniel sends Matilda a note saying he is safe at ___'s house.

15. SFROT = 15. _____
    It kills off the mosquitoes and the yellow fever.

16. ROYWD =16. _____
Joseph thinks Matilda should sell the coffeehouse so she has a nice ___.

17. RSTIK =17. _____
Matilda uses this to try to catch fish.

18. NSXGTOBRO =18. _____
Hiding place for coffeehouse money

19. LGGFA =19. _____
Grandfather flirts with her as she nurses Matilda back to health.

20. AONGW =20. _____
Transportation to the country

21. SRPAE =21. _____
Matilda is gathering these when she passes out, sick with the fever

22. FEHRCN =22. _____
These doctors know how to treat the fever better than anyone else.

23. EIGLVIO =23. _____
Family Matilda's mother hopes her daughter can marry into

24. TEMOHR =24. _____
She is assumed dead but comes back to the coffeehouse at the end.

25. EDBBOR =25. _____
Matilda and her grandfather return to Philadelphia & discover they were ___.

26. RHCNU =26. _____
Chore to keep the children busy: ___ butter

27. LEEOTCT =27. _____
Eloped with her French tutor

28. LKAW =28. _____
What Matilda and Nathaniel do every evening

29. DWSTAUS =29. _____
People mixed it with flour to make more bread.

30. LLESB =30. _____
These ring whenever someone dies.

31. LLOPY =31. _____
Girl who worked at the coffeehouse who dies of yellow fever

32. TOCRUYN =32. _____
Wealthy people flee there to escape the fever.

33. ROPATTIR =33. _____
Item Matilda buries with her grandfather

34. RTAHFE =34. _____
He fell off a ladder and died of a broken neck.

35. LIBEB =35. _____
Matilda likes to read it at the end of each day.

36. SREFOLW =36. _____
Nathaniel Benson throws these out a window at Matilda and Eliza.

37. HGNOSIWNTA =37. _____
Business grows when George ___ builds a home a few blocks away.

38. OWILLW =38. _____
Matilda searches for this kind of a tree, knowing water will be nearby.

39. SDORW =39. _____
Matilda stabs the robber with it.

40. SHBU =40. _____
Matilda is taken to ___ Hill to recover from yellow fever.

41. ELNL =41. _____
Small child Matilda finds and cares for

42. IPENTAR =42. _____
Nathaniel Benson's job

43. RNNADSEO =43. _____
Author

JUGGLE LETTERS ANSWER KEY - Fever 1793

1. LSISA = 1. SILAS
   The cat's name

2. PSHEJO = 2. JOSEPH
   Eliza's brother who lost his wife to yellow fever

3. IGLOTUDNN = 3. LUDINGTON
   Family whose farm Matilda's mother wants to send her to

4. TRAEMK = 4. MARKET
   Place where people buy and sell food

5. HASWVRE = 5. WHARVES
   Matilda's mother forbids her to go there for fear she might get sick.

6. ILAZE = 6. ELIZA
   Coffeehouse partner with Matilda

7. GAOEPANRH = 7. ORPHANAGE
   Place the people at Bush Hill want Matilda to go to help out

8. DNEGAR = 8. GARDEN
   Place Matilda's grandfather wants her to get their food

9. ADRIGR = 9. GIRARD
   Stephen ___ turns Bush Hill into a safe hospital.

10. RCTA =10. CART
    A man dumps Matilda's mother off of one.

11. EFRJEFNSO =11. JEFFERSON
    Matilda wants to get Thomas ___ to eat at the coffeehouse.

12. SRHU =12. RUSH
    He believes black people can't catch yellow fever.

13. EUSGFEER =13. REFUGEES
    People Matilda's grandfather thinks are to blame for the fever

14. LAEEP =14. PEALE
    Nathaniel sends Matilda a note saying he is safe at ___'s house.

15. SFROT =15. FROST
    It kills off the mosquitoes and the yellow fever.

16. ROYWD =16. DOWRY
Joseph thinks Matilda should sell the coffeehouse so she has a nice ___.

17. RSTIK =17. SKIRT
Matilda uses this to try to catch fish.

18. NSXGTOBRO =18. STRONGBOX
Hiding place for coffeehouse money

19. LGGFA =19. FLAGG
Grandfather flirts with her as she nurses Matilda back to health.

20. AONGW =20. WAGON
Transportation to the country

20. SRPAE =20. PEARS
Matilda is gathering these when she passes out, sick with the fever

21. FEHRCN =21. FRENCH
These doctors know how to treat the fever better than anyone else.

22. EIGLVIO =22. OGILVIE
Family Matilda's mother hopes her daughter can marry into

23. TEMOHR =23. MOTHER
She is assumed dead but comes back to the coffeehouse at the end.

24. EDBBOR =24. ROBBED
Matilda and her grandfather return to Philadelphia & discover they were ___.

25. RHCNU =25. CHURN
Chore to keep the children busy: ___ butter

26. LEEOTCT =26. COLETTE
Eloped with her French tutor

27. LKAW =27. WALK
What Matilda and Nathaniel do every evening

28. DWSTAUS =28. SAWDUST
People mixed it with flour to make more bread.

29. LLESB =29. BELLS
These ring whenever someone dies.

30. LLOPY =30. POLLY
Girl who worked at the coffeehouse who dies of yellow fever

31. TOCRUYN =31. COUNTRY
Wealthy people flee there to escape the fever.

32. ROPATTIR =32. PORTRAIT
Item Matilda buries with her grandfather

33. RTAHFE =33. FATHER
He fell off a ladder and died of a broken neck.

34. LIBEB =34. BIBLE
Matilda likes to read it at the end of each day.

35. SREFOLW =35. FLOWERS
Nathaniel Benson throws these out a window at Matilda and Eliza.

36. HGNOSIWNTA =36. WASHINGTON
Business grows when George ___ builds a home a few blocks away.

37. OWILLW =37. WILLOW
Matilda searches for this kind of a tree, knowing water will be nearby.

38. SDORW =38. SWORD
Matilda stabs the robber with it.

39. SHBU =39. BUSH
Matilda is taken to ___ Hill to recover from yellow fever.

40. ELNL =40. NELL
Small child Matilda finds and cares for

41. IPENTAR =41. PAINTER
Nathaniel Benson's job

42. RNNADSEO =42. ANDERSON
Author

VOCABULARY RESOURCE MATERIALS

Fever 1793 Vocabulary Word List

No.	Word	Clue/Definition
1.	ABHORRED	Detested utterly; loathed; hated
2.	ABIDE	Tolerate; put up with; stay
3.	AILS	Causes physical or emotional pain
4.	BEGRUDGE	Envy or resent the good fortune of someone else
5.	BESTIR	Stir up; rouse; bring to action
6.	BILIOUS	Extremely unpleasant or distasteful in regards to sickness
7.	BRANDISH	Shake or wave a weapon
8.	BUNKUM	Insincere or ridiculous talk
9.	CACKLED	Voiced a shrill, broken laugh
10.	CAJOLING	Persuading with flattery or promises
11.	COMMOTION	Disturbance; chaotic activity
12.	CONCEDED	Yielded; admitted; relinquished; reluctantly acknowledged
13.	DEMURE	Shy; modest; coy
14.	DESTITUTE	Lacking food, clothing, and shelter; without necessities
15.	DIM	Not bright; dull
16.	DISENTANGLING	Unravelling; becoming free from
17.	DROLL	Amusing or funny in an odd or dry way
18.	EXORBITANT	Excessive; extreme; unreasonable
19.	EXTINGUISH	Put out or bring to an end
20.	FAMISHED	Extremely hungry
21.	FATIGUE	Weariness from bodily or mental exhaustion
22.	FETID	Having an offensive odor
23.	FORGE	Workshop of a blacksmith
24.	GAUNT	Extremely thin and bony
25.	GUMPTION	Aggressiveness; boldness
26.	HARRUMPHED	Offered brief, critical comments
27.	HASTE	Swiftness of motion; hurry; rush
28.	HOISTED	Lifted; raised up
29.	IMPLORE	Beg urgently
30.	IMPUDENCE	Quality of being offensively bold; nerve; rudeness
31.	INSTILL	Gradually put something into someone's mind or feelings
32.	INVALID	Someone too weak to care for himself
33.	JAUNDICED	Having a yellow discoloration of the skin due to disease
34.	LOITERING	Lingering aimlessly; hanging about with no purpose
35.	MELODIOUS	Sweet-sounding
36.	MIASMA	Poisonous fumes or germs polluting the atmosphere
37.	PESTILENCE	A deadly disease
38.	PLACID	Quiet; calm; peaceful
39.	PROPRIETOR	Owner of a business establishment
40.	PURGE	Cleanse; purify
41.	PUTRID	Rotten; decaying
42.	RELENT	Slacken; abandon; withdraw; give in
43.	RESOLUTELY	Firmly determined
44.	RUCKUS	Noisy commotion or disturbance
45.	SALVAGE	Save; rescue
46.	SCURRILOUS	Obscene; vulgar; abusive
47.	SHROUD	Cloth or sheet wrapping a corpse
48.	SNIPPET	Small or insignificant person
49.	SOLEMN	Serious; not to be taken lightly
50.	SOLITARY	Alone or unattended
51.	TAUT	Tightly drawn; tense 177

No.	Word	Clue/Definition
51.	TAUT	Tightly drawn; tense
52.	TETHERED	Attached by a short rope
53.	TRIFLING	Small; of little importance
54.	TRUNDLED	Moved along
55.	VANITY	Excessive pride in one's appearance
56.	VEHEMENTLY	With great passion or energy
57.	VENTURING	Taking a risk or braving dangers
58.	VICTUALS	Food fit for humans to eat
59.	WEARILY	In a fatigued, tired, or worn-out way
60.	WHARVES	Landing places where ships may tie up to load or unload

VOCABULARY WORD SEARCH - Fever 1793

```
A B I D E T S I O H D E M U R E P R B
M B I Q C X G B X X C U V C E R U E U
S M H W V V O S S N L G E A L O T S N
A G S O T B S R E W T I N C E L R O K
I A O B R L I D B U T T K N P I L U
M U L P I R U N A I P A U L T M D U M
G N I A C P E T S R T F R E M I M T S
U T T J M D X D O T Z A I D H X S E U
M J A I S Z G P B Z I L N G A H G L O
P D R M L O R I P P P L G T R M N Y L
T E Y G N I L O J A C O L O R S I S I
I B S L E I H E R X E R U R U R R N R
O J Z T O R A W M X G D G K M C E I R
N B O U I K S B E N D M C W P Q T P U
P R S G K L T B D A U U R F H S I P C
S A L V A G E Z D E R E H T E T O E S
F O R G E G W N L M G I J B D T L T N
T W H A R V E S C S E Z L V A N I T Y
B T R U N D L E D E B L W Y R K Q D C
B S P L A C I D E X T I N G U I S H D
```

ABHORRED	DIM	HASTE	PURGE	SOLITARY
ABIDE	DROLL	HOISTED	PUTRID	TAUT
AILS	EXORBITANT	IMPLORE	RELENT	TETHERED
BEGRUDGE	EXTINGUISH	IMPUDENCE	RESOLUTELY	TRUNDLED
BESTIR	FATIGUE	INSTILL	RUCKUS	VANITY
BILIOUS	FETID	LOITERING	SALVAGE	VENTURING
BUNKUM	FORGE	MIASMA	SCURRILOUS	WEARILY
CACKLED	GAUNT	PESTILENCE	SHROUD	WHARVES
CAJOLING	GUMPTION	PLACID	SNIPPET	
DEMURE	HARRUMPHED	PROPRIETOR	SOLEMN	

VOCABULARY WORD SEARCH ANSWER KEY - Fever 1793

```
A B I D E T S I O H D E M U R E P R B
M B I     X         C U V C E R U E U
S M H S   O   N     G E A L O T R N
A G S O   R E   T   I N C E L P R O K
I A O R L I D B U   T K N E P I O U
M U L I R U N A I P A U K E T M L M
G N T A P E T S R T F R E   I U S
U T   M   D O T   A I D H   T E U
M A   I   S P B I L N   H A   G L O
P R       O R I       G T R   N Y I L
T Y G N I L O J A C O L O R S I S I
I S   E I H E     E R U   R E   N R R
O T   A W M G D   K M   E T   P U
N O U   S   E N D     C P   T   P C
R S   L T         A U   F H S I   E S
S A L V A G E     D E R E H T E T O E S
F O R G E G   N       G I   B D T L T
  W H A R V E S C     E   L V A N I T Y
    T R U N D L E D E B     Y       D
      P L A C I D E X T I N G U I S H
```

ABHORRED	DIM	HASTE	PURGE	SOLITARY
ABIDE	DROLL	HOISTED	PUTRID	TAUT
AILS	EXORBITANT	IMPLORE	RELENT	TETHERED
BEGRUDGE	EXTINGUISH	IMPUDENCE	RESOLUTELY	TRUNDLED
BESTIR	FATIGUE	INSTILL	RUCKUS	VANITY
BILIOUS	FETID	LOITERING	SALVAGE	VENTURING
BUNKUM	FORGE	MIASMA	SCURRILOUS	WEARILY
CACKLED	GAUNT	PESTILENCE	SHROUD	WHARVES
CAJOLING	GUMPTION	PLACID	SNIPPET	
DEMURE	HARRUMPHED	PROPRIETOR	SOLEMN	

VOCABULARY CROSSWORD - Fever 1793

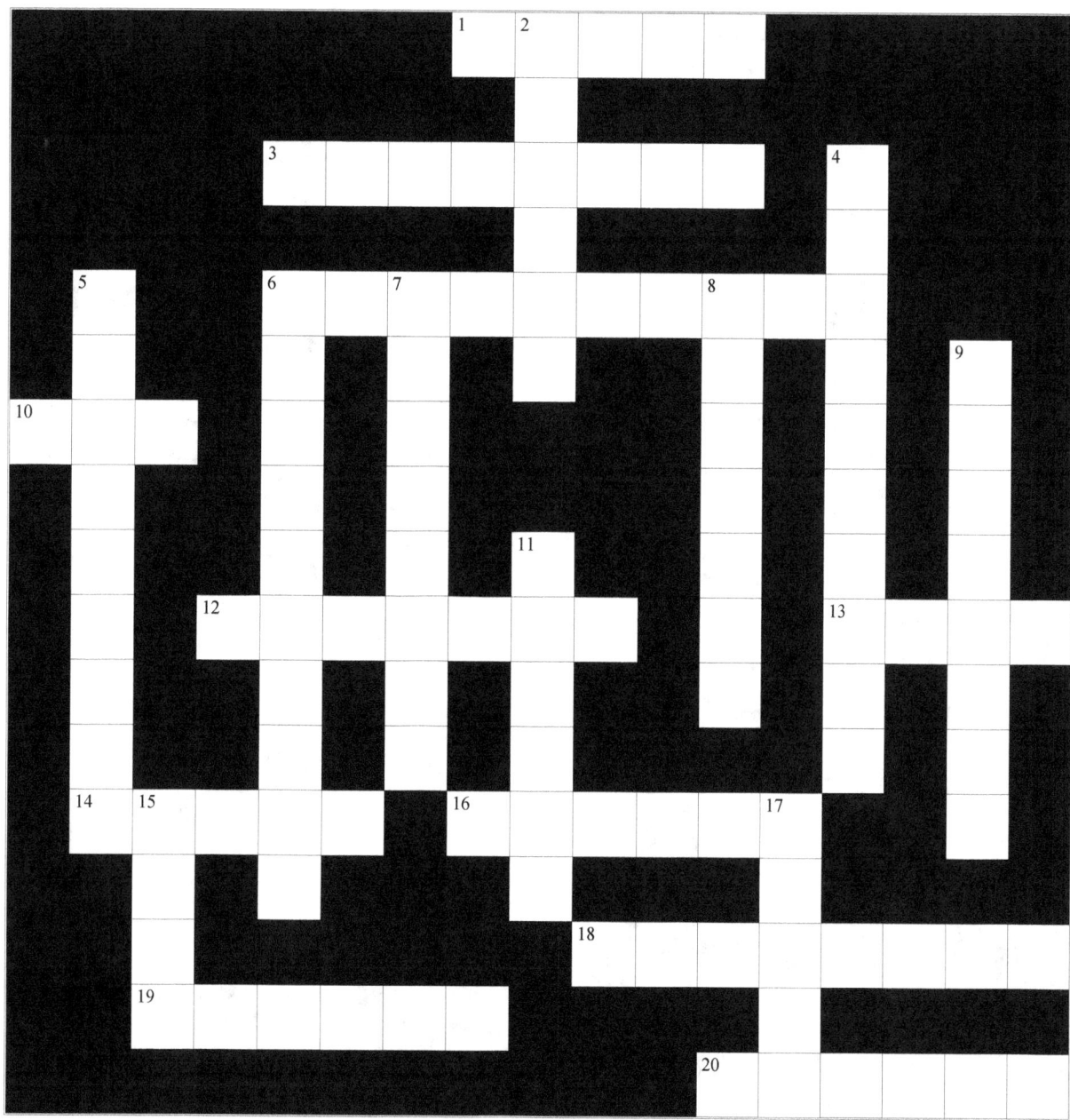

Across
1. Amusing or funny in an odd or dry way
3. Persuading with flattery or promises
6. Put out or bring to an end
10. Not bright; dull
12. Extremely unpleasant or distasteful in regards to sickness
13. Tightly drawn; tense
14. Extremely thin and bony
16. Poisonous fumes or germs polluting the atmosphere
18. Alone or unattended
19. Serious; not to be taken lightly
20. Shy; modest; coy

Down
2. Slacken; abandon; withdraw; give in
4. With great passion or energy
5. Lingering aimlessly; hanging about with no purpose
6. Excessive; extreme; unreasonable
7. Small; of little importance
8. Someone too weak to care for himself
9. Envy or resent the good fortune of someone else
11. Rotten; decaying
15. Causes physical or emotional pain
17. Tolerate; put up with; stay

VOCABULARY CROSSWORD ANSWER KEY - Fever 1793

Across
1. Amusing or funny in an odd or dry way
3. Persuading with flattery or promises
6. Put out or bring to an end
10. Not bright; dull
12. Extremely unpleasant or distasteful in regards to sickness
13. Tightly drawn; tense
14. Extremely thin and bony
16. Poisonous fumes or germs polluting the atmosphere
18. Alone or unattended
19. Serious; not to be taken lightly
20. Shy; modest; coy

Down
2. Slacken; abandon; withdraw; give in
4. With great passion or energy
5. Lingering aimlessly; hanging about with no purpose
6. Excessive; extreme; unreasonable
7. Small; of little importance
8. Someone too weak to care for himself
9. Envy or resent the good fortune of someone else
11. Rotten; decaying
15. Causes physical or emotional pain
17. Tolerate; put up with; stay

MATCHING 1 - Fever 1793

___ 1. FETID   A. Not bright; dull
___ 2. JAUNDICED   B. Insincere or ridiculous talk
___ 3. SOLEMN   C. Cloth or sheet wrapping a corpse
___ 4. IMPUDENCE   D. Quiet; calm; peaceful
___ 5. SHROUD   E. Firmly determined
___ 6. RUCKUS   F. Offered brief, critical comments
___ 7. HASTE   G. Shake or wave a weapon
___ 8. BUNKUM   H. Small; of little importance
___ 9. EXORBITANT   I. Tolerate; put up with; stay
___10. PLACID   J. Noisy commotion or disturbance
___11. BRANDISH   K. Lingering aimlessly; hanging about with no purpose
___12. LOITERING   L. Excessive; extreme; unreasonable
___13. VENTURING   M. A deadly disease
___14. TRIFLING   N. Having an offensive odor
___15. RESOLUTELY   O. Serious; not to be taken lightly
___16. MIASMA   P. Save; rescue
___17. HARRUMPHED   Q. Excessive pride in one's appearance
___18. PESTILENCE   R. Lacking food, clothing, and shelter; without necessities
___19. ABIDE   S. Swiftness of motion; hurry; rush
___20. DESTITUTE   T. Taking a risk or braving dangers
___21. FAMISHED   U. Quality of being offensively bold; nerve; rudeness
___22. AILS   V. Extremely hungry
___23. VANITY   W. Poisonous fumes or germs polluting the atmosphere
___24. DIM   X. Causes physical or emotional pain
___25. SALVAGE   Y. Having a yellow discoloration of the skin due to disease

MATCHING 1 ANSWER KEY - Fever 1793

N - 1. FETID   A. Not bright; dull
Y - 2. JAUNDICED   B. Insincere or ridiculous talk
O - 3. SOLEMN   C. Cloth or sheet wrapping a corpse
U - 4. IMPUDENCE   D. Quiet; calm; peaceful
C - 5. SHROUD   E. Firmly determined
J - 6. RUCKUS   F. Offered brief, critical comments
S - 7. HASTE   G. Shake or wave a weapon
B - 8. BUNKUM   H. Small; of little importance
L - 9. EXORBITANT   I. Tolerate; put up with; stay
D -10. PLACID   J. Noisy commotion or disturbance
G -11. BRANDISH   K. Lingering aimlessly; hanging about with no purpose
K -12. LOITERING   L. Excessive; extreme; unreasonable
T -13. VENTURING   M. A deadly disease
H -14. TRIFLING   N. Having an offensive odor
E -15. RESOLUTELY   O. Serious; not to be taken lightly
W 16. MIASMA   P. Save; rescue
F -17. HARRUMPHED   Q. Excessive pride in one's appearance
M ·18. PESTILENCE   R. Lacking food, clothing, and shelter; without necessities
I - 19. ABIDE   S. Swiftness of motion; hurry; rush
R -20. DESTITUTE   T. Taking a risk or braving dangers
V -21. FAMISHED   U. Quality of being offensively bold; nerve; rudeness
X -22. AILS   V. Extremely hungry
Q -23. VANITY   W. Poisonous fumes or germs polluting the atmosphere
A -24. DIM   X. Causes physical or emotional pain
P -25. SALVAGE   Y. Having a yellow discoloration of the skin due to disease

VOCABULARY MATCHING 2 - Fever 1793

___ 1. HARRUMPHED   A. Tightly drawn; tense

___ 2. BRANDISH   B. Unravelling; becoming free from

___ 3. SOLEMN   C. Causes physical or emotional pain

___ 4. FAMISHED   D. Offered brief, critical comments

___ 5. INVALID   E. Lifted; raised up

___ 6. FETID   F. Shake or wave a weapon

___ 7. TAUT   G. Someone too weak to care for himself

___ 8. IMPLORE   H. Serious; not to be taken lightly

___ 9. COMMOTION   I. Having an offensive odor

___ 10. CAJOLING   J. Firmly determined

___ 11. MELODIOUS   K. Not bright; dull

___ 12. INSTILL   L. Extremely hungry

___ 13. EXTINGUISH   M. Persuading with flattery or promises

___ 14. IMPUDENCE   N. Noisy commotion or disturbance

___ 15. RESOLUTELY   O. Moved along

___ 16. LOITERING   P. Envy or resent the good fortune of someone else

___ 17. AILS   Q. Sweet-sounding

___ 18. VEHEMENTLY   R. With great passion or energy

___ 19. BEGRUDGE   S. Put out or bring to an end

___ 20. DISENTANGLING   T. Lingering aimlessly; hanging about with no purpose

___ 21. RUCKUS   U. Quality of being offensively bold; nerve; rudeness

___ 22. HOISTED   V. Voiced a shrill, broken laugh

___ 23. TRUNDLED   W. Disturbance; chaotic activity

___ 24. DIM   X. Gradually put something into someone's mind or feelings

___ 25. CACKLED   Y. Beg urgently

VOCABULARY MATCHING ANSWER KEY - Fever 1793

D - 1. HARRUMPHED	A. Tightly drawn; tense
F - 2. BRANDISH	B. Unravelling; becoming free from
H - 3. SOLEMN	C. Causes physical or emotional pain
L - 4. FAMISHED	D. Offered brief, critical comments
G - 5. INVALID	E. Lifted; raised up
I - 6. FETID	F. Shake or wave a weapon
A - 7. TAUT	G. Someone too weak to care for himself
Y - 8. IMPLORE	H. Serious; not to be taken lightly
W - 9. COMMOTION	I. Having an offensive odor
M - 10. CAJOLING	J. Firmly determined
Q - 11. MELODIOUS	K. Not bright; dull
X - 12. INSTILL	L. Extremely hungry
S - 13. EXTINGUISH	M. Persuading with flattery or promises
U - 14. IMPUDENCE	N. Noisy commotion or disturbance
J - 15. RESOLUTELY	O. Moved along
T - 16. LOITERING	P. Envy or resent the good fortune of someone else
C - 17. AILS	Q. Sweet-sounding
R - 18. VEHEMENTLY	R. With great passion or energy
P - 19. BEGRUDGE	S. Put out or bring to an end
B - 20. DISENTANGLING	T. Lingering aimlessly; hanging about with no purpose
N - 21. RUCKUS	U. Quality of being offensively bold; nerve; rudeness
E - 22. HOISTED	V. Voiced a shrill, broken laugh
O - 23. TRUNDLED	W. Disturbance; chaotic activity
K - 24. DIM	X. Gradually put something into someone's mind or feelings
V - 25. CACKLED	Y. Beg urgently

VOCABULARY JUGGLE LETTERS - Fever 1793

1. CLIDPA = 1. _____
   Quiet; calm; peaceful

2. ISAL = 2. _____
   Causes physical or emotional pain

3. DUHORS = 3. _____
   Cloth or sheet wrapping a corpse

4. INJGLCAO = 4. _____
   Persuading with flattery or promises

5. ULCRORUSSI = 5. _____
   Obscene; vulgar; abusive

6. ETERTHDE = 6. _____
   Attached by a short rope

7. GUPER = 7. _____
   Cleanse; purify

8. EFDTI = 8. _____
   Having an offensive odor

9. URBEDEGG = 9. _____
   Envy or resent the good fortune of someone else

10. NISLTIL =10. _____
    Gradually put something into someone's mind or feelings

11. CEMEDPNUI =11. _____
    Quality of being offensively bold; nerve; rudeness

12. IATSCVUL =12. _____
    Food fit for humans to eat

13. HDARMHERPU =13. _____
    Offered brief, critical comments

14. OTSYAIRL =14. _____
    Alone or unattended

15. SEDITOH =15. _____
    Lifted; raised up

16. EFROG =16. _____
Workshop of a blacksmith

17. EBIAD =17. _____
Tolerate; put up with; stay

18. TUGAN =18. _____
Extremely thin and bony

19. DECDNCOE =19. _____
Yielded; admitted; relinquished; reluctantly acknowledged

20. LAEGVAS =20. _____
Save; rescue

21. AAMMSI =21. _____
Poisonous fumes or germs polluting the atmosphere

22. TTXIEOBRNA =22. _____
Excessive; extreme; unreasonable

23. LIUISBO =23. _____
Extremely unpleasant or distasteful in regards to sickness

24. EIRBST =24. _____
Stir up; rouse; bring to action

25. URDMEE =25. _____
Shy; modest; coy

26. DBNRASIH =26. _____
Shake or wave a weapon

27. SEMLUODIO =27. _____
Sweet-sounding

28. ROPEMIL =28. _____
Beg urgently

29. OEEYLUTRLS =29. _____
Firmly determined

30. NSGHXUTIIE =30. _____
Put out or bring to an end

31. UDTISTETE =31. _____
Lacking food, clothing, and shelter; without necessities

32. GINSGIANENDLT =32. _____
Unravelling; becoming free from

33. NIRTLGFI =33. _____
Small; of little importance

34. NUREGVTNI =34. _____
Taking a risk or braving dangers

35. ROIOPERTPR =35. _____
Owner of a business establishment

36. NDLRDEUT =36. _____
Moved along

37. LRDOL =37. _____
Amusing or funny in an odd or dry way

38. ACKCLED =38. _____
Voiced a shrill, broken laugh

39. SHWARVE =39. _____
Landing places where ships may tie up to load or unload

40. EPNTSIECEL =40. _____
A deadly disease

41. LYWIREA =41. _____
In a fatigued, tired, or worn-out way

42. IOPMNGUT =42. _____
Aggressiveness; boldness

43. EPSNPIT =43. _____
Small or insignificant person

44. IOMONCOMT =44. _____
Disturbance; chaotic activity

45. UIFEAGT =45. _____
Weariness from bodily or mental exhaustion

46. IDM =46. _____
Not bright; dull

VOCABULARY JUGGLE LETTERS ANSWER KEY - Fever 1793

1. CLIDPA = 1. PLACID
   Quiet; calm; peaceful

2. ISAL = 2. AILS
   Causes physical or emotional pain

3. DUHORS = 3. SHROUD
   Cloth or sheet wrapping a corpse

4. INJGLCAO = 4. CAJOLING
   Persuading with flattery or promises

5. ULCRORUSSI = 5. SCURRILOUS
   Obscene; vulgar; abusive

6. ETERTHDE = 6. TETHERED
   Attached by a short rope

7. GUPER = 7. PURGE
   Cleanse; purify

8. EFDTI = 8. FETID
   Having an offensive odor

9. URBEDEGG = 9. BEGRUDGE
   Envy or resent the good fortune of someone else

10. NISLTIL = 10. INSTILL
    Gradually put something into someone's mind or feelings

11. CEMEDPNUI = 11. IMPUDENCE
    Quality of being offensively bold; nerve; rudeness

12. IATSCVUL = 12. VICTUALS
    Food fit for humans to eat

13. HDARMHERPU = 13. HARRUMPHED
    Offered brief, critical comments

14. OTSYAIRL = 14. SOLITARY
    Alone or unattended

15. SEDITOH = 15. HOISTED
    Lifted; raised up

16. EFROG =16. FORGE
Workshop of a blacksmith

17. EBIAD =17. ABIDE
Tolerate; put up with; stay

18. TUGAN =18. GAUNT
Extremely thin and bony

19. DECDNCOE =19. CONCEDED
Yielded; admitted; relinquished; reluctantly acknowledged

20. LAEGVAS =20. SALVAGE
Save; rescue

21. AAMMSI =21. MIASMA
Poisonous fumes or germs polluting the atmosphere

22. TTXIEOBRNA =22. EXORBITANT
Excessive; extreme; unreasonable

23. LIUISBO =23. BILIOUS
Extremely unpleasant or distasteful in regards to sickness

24. EIRBST =24. BESTIR
Stir up; rouse; bring to action

25. URDMEE =25. DEMURE
Shy; modest; coy

26. DBNRASIH =26. BRANDISH
Shake or wave a weapon

27. SEMLUODIO =27. MELODIOUS
Sweet-sounding

28. ROPEMIL =28. IMPLORE
Beg urgently

29. OEEYLUTRLS =29. RESOLUTELY
Firmly determined

30. NSGHXUTIIE =30. EXTINGUISH
Put out or bring to an end

31. UDTISTETE =31. DESTITUTE
Lacking food, clothing, and shelter; without necessities

32. GINSGIANENDLT =32. DISENTANGLING
Unravelling; becoming free from

33. NIRTLGFI =33. TRIFLING
Small; of little importance

34. NUREGVTNI =34. VENTURING
Taking a risk or braving dangers

35. ROIOPERTPR =35. PROPRIETOR
Owner of a business establishment

36. NDLRDEUT =36. TRUNDLED
Moved along

37. LRDOL =37. DROLL
Amusing or funny in an odd or dry way

38. ACKCLED =38. CACKLED
Voiced a shrill, broken laugh

39. SHWARVE =39. WHARVES
Landing places where ships may tie up to load or unload

40. EPNTSIECEL =40. PESTILENCE
A deadly disease

41. LYWIREA =41. WEARILY
In a fatigued, tired, or worn-out way

42. IOPMNGUT =42. GUMPTION
Aggressiveness; boldness

43. EPSNPIT =43. SNIPPET
Small or insignificant person

44. IOMONCOMT =44. COMMOTION
Disturbance; chaotic activity

45. UIFEAGT =45. FATIGUE
Weariness from bodily or mental exhaustion

46. IDM =46. DIM
Not bright; dull